MUST WE DEFEND NAZIS?

MUST WE DEFEND NAZIS?

Why the
First Amendment
Should Not Protect
Hate Speech and
White Supremacy

RICHARD DELGADO

&

JEAN STEFANCIC

NEW YORK UNIVERSITY PRESS

New York

NEW YORK UNIVERSITY PRESS
New York
www.nyupress.org
© 2018 by New York University
All rights reserved

Book designed and typeset by Charles B. Hames

References to Internet websites (URLs) were accurate at the time of
writing. Neither the author nor New York University Press is
responsible for URLs that may have expired or changed
since the manuscript was prepared.

ISBN: 978-1-4798-8771-2 (hardback)
ISBN: 978-1-4798-5783-8 (paperback)

For Library of Congress Cataloging-in-Publication data,
please contact the Library of Congress.

New York University Press books are printed on acid-free paper,
and their binding materials are chosen for strength and durability.
We strive to use environmentally responsible suppliers and materials to
the greatest extent possible in publishing our books.

Manufactured in the United States of America

10 9 8 7 6 5 4 3 2 1

Also available as an ebook

CONTENTS

PREFACE

Should Nazis, white supremacists, and Ku Klux Klan members spewing hatred be allowed to march in a peaceful college town like Charlottesville, Virginia? Should city officials give them a permit, and should the local police provide them with protection from indignant protesters?

If trouble erupts, as it easily might in such situations, and the case ends up in court, the ACLU, which champions both the First Amendment and the rights of minorities—blacks, LGBT people, Latinos, Muslims, and Jews—might easily find itself called to defend the marchers, as it has done in the past. Is this logically necessary, or wise?

If a neo-Nazi sympathizer who has driven to the rally fueled by hate runs over a crowd of peaceful protesters, killing one and injuring many others, should the president of the United States condemn both sides as equally culpable?

What about members of a fringe religious group who vent their displeasure against homosexuals by staging a noisy demonstration at the funeral of a war veteran? Though they are not injuring anybody or threatening violent harm, they are disturbing the sanctity of the event and the feelings of the bereaved attenders. The authorities might be tempted to ask them to move on. Yet, their demonstration took place on a public street and was an attempt, however misguided, to bring the question of homosexuality to public attention. Must society allow them to do so?

Once again hate speech—words that wound—has vaulted to public attention in a host of settings, including college campuses, demonstrations, the Internet, talk radio, and even presidential addresses and campaign rallies. The First Amendment protects speech as a prime value and considers it a democracy-enhancing instrument and protector of communal decision-making. Yet hateful speech, especially the racial kind, can shock and wound, rending its victims speechless, afraid, and silent, less able to participate in public conversation than they were before being made to suffer it.

Defenders of free-speech rights, such as the ACLU, are fond of saying that we must protect "the speech we hate" in order to safeguard that which we love. Presumably they mean political speech or words that criticize a public official for his or her performance. But is it really so hard to distinguish between the hateful kind and that which we all desire to protect?

Is this any harder than, for example, figuring out which kinds of *associational* rights we want to protect—the Girl Scouts meeting to discuss wildlife protection or first aid, certainly, but not criminals or terrorists meeting in secret to plan their next move?

Or put it this way: must the First Amendment be a seamless web, as many seem to think it is? It never has been and it is not now. For decades, courts have held that hate speech on the job can amount to employment discrimination, which is of course illegal. And if you employ too much vituperation on the Internet you may find that your service provider cuts you off, which it is entirely within its province to do. In many court systems, hate speech is a tort for which one can recover damages in a civil lawsuit. And for several years, federal authorities have been punishing hate *crime* when someone commits an offense, such as assault or arson, with a racial motivation—which is of course provable only by examining what the accused has said or posted somewhere, perhaps on the Internet.

For many years, courts have been redressing hate speech under a variety of existing causes of action, even if they do not fit exactly. For example, the offending words might have been overheard and so amount to a borderline defamation. A court might easily find that they contain an element of menace or threat, and if so amount to an assault or battery, especially if they accompany light touching, a push, or a shove.

What if they lack any of these, but the victim of those harsh, racially tinged words is a schoolchild and the speaker is a teacher, administrator, or other authority? Once again, courts seem willing to try to find a theory to justify relief, even though no statute or express common-law cause of action commands it.

Other countries go even further, punishing hate speech as a crime, particularly if it targets historically oppressed groups such as Jews or Roma (Gypsies). The sky doesn't fall: indeed many of these countries have a political atmosphere that is freer and more vibrant than ours; citizens there merely cannot engage in vituperation against each other. So why are we so reluctant to follow suit?

If hate speech is not a legal wrong, is it nevertheless immoral, so that we all should condemn it and not make special efforts to "defend Nazis," in the words of our title? Perhaps not—maybe abrasive speech is merely part of the ordinary give-and-take of daily life, something we all should get used to and ignore. Or learn to talk back. Or be grateful when it happens because it enables us to know who thinks ill of us and who doesn't. At the time we went to press, the ACLU was struggling with these very questions in connection with white supremacist rallies like the one mentioned above, especially those that include guns.

Defenders of a vigorous system of free speech often encourage the victims of hate speech to "get over it." They dismiss their reactions to hate speech as mere offense, as though it were a matter of being called by the wrong name in class or at a work meeting. Indeed, how damaging is hate speech? Does it cause lasting injury, and, if so, of what kind? Who is most vulnerable—children? Minorities? Workers in an office laced with homophobic or misogynistic remarks and "jokes"?

◆ ◆ ◆

This book takes up all these issues. Chapter 1 considers the harms of hate speech. Chapter 2 examines hate speech on university and college campuses. Chapter 3 discusses hate speech in an emerging realm—cyberspace. Chapter 4 analyzes arguments against hate-speech regulation that tend to be associated with neoliberals. Chapter 5 takes up a number of arguments made by neoconservatives. Chapter 6 examines the experiences of other Western societies that have enacted anti-hate-speech laws to see what lessons they offer for American institutions. Chapter 7 sets out guides for activist lawyers and judges interested in approaching the hate-speech controversy intelligently. A final chapter discusses "the speech we hate."

As we'll see, this book argues for a much more nuanced position than the one you usually hear. We believe that society should take more decisive measures to marginalize and discourage hate speech of all kinds than it has been doing. Moreover, we believe that this would be constitutionally and morally permissible and the right thing to do, even in the world of business and profits, such as the Internet.

Is this book—and the slow turn whose development it traces—bad news for lovers of free expression and debate? Not at all. For one thing, it can hardly serve the defenders of any system of values to pretend that the system is not in need of reform if it really is. For another, we argue that mechanical jurisprudence has seemingly paralyzed the thinking of many First Amendment absolutists. Judging from the naïve policy arguments they continue to put forward, their mental muscles have been paralyzed through disuse. Alerting them to the kind of debate they must now enter benefits them as well as society at large.

This book points out that values of free expression and equal dignity stand in reciprocal relation. The civil rights struggle relies on speech and expression. Equality, in short, presupposes speech. And conversely, any sort of meaningful speech requires equal dignity, equal access, and equal respect on the part of all who participate in a dialogue. Free speech, in other words, presupposes equality. Adjusting the fine balance between these two seemingly incompatible values can only strengthen both.

The time has come for our finest minds—and for citizens at large—to understand the double dependency between free speech and equal dignity, and to realize that the hard work of balancing competing principles must now begin. It is imperative to put aside tired maxims and conversation-closing clichés that formerly cluttered First Amendment thinking and case law. With the belief that this hard work will prove to be beneficial, not only for marginalized groups struggling against a tide of injurious depiction but for an increasingly diverse society at large, we wrote this book.

1

THE HARMS OF HATE SPEECH

A prime obstacle to re-forming hate-speech law is the insistence by some that these forms of speech are harmless or that tolerating them is "the price we pay" for living in a free society. This chapter provides evidence that they are not at all harmless, and that free-speech ideology needs to change to recognize and deal with the harms they produce.

In *Snyder v. Phelps* (the Westboro Baptist Church case), a group of marchers from a fringe organization gathered on the street outside a funeral service being held to honor a war veteran in Maryland. Their protest had little to do with the war or the particular veteran who died in it. Instead, they picketed and marched to protest the American public's increasing acceptance of homosexuality, which they considered a sin. Deeply upset by what he considered the desecration of a solemn moment, the veteran's father sued for intentional infliction of emotional distress, defamation, and a few other counts. He described that he had become upset, tearful, angry, and physically nauseated to the point that he had to vomit. He stated that the defendants had rendered him unable to think of his son without thinking of the protesters' actions, adding, "I want so badly to remember all the good stuff . . . but it always turns into the bad." Several expert witnesses testified that the defendants' behavior had worsened Phelps's diabetes and caused him to sink into depression.

A jury awarded him a considerable sum, but the Court of Appeals and Supreme Court reversed on the ground that the picketers' speech concerned a matter (treatment of homosexuals) of public interest and took place on public property—the street.

Earlier, in *Contreras v. Crown Zellerbach*, the Washington Supreme Court had held that a Mexican American's allegations that fellow employees had subjected him to a campaign of racial abuse stated a valid claim against his employer for the tort of outrage (an alternative name for the tort of infliction of emotional distress). The plaintiff alleged that he had suffered "humiliation and embarrassment by reason of racial jokes, slurs and comments" and that the defendant's agents and employees had wrongfully accused him of stealing the employer's property, thereby preventing him from gaining employment and holding him up to public ridicule. Focusing on the racial abuse, the court declared that "racial epithets which were once part of common usage may not now be looked upon as mere insulting language."

Only eleven months later, however, the U.S. Court of Appeals for the Seventh Circuit in *Collins v. Smith* affirmed a federal district court's decision declaring unconstitutional certain ordinances of the village of Skokie, Illinois, that had been drafted to block a demonstration by members of the National Socialist Party of America. The village argued that the demonstration, together with the display of Nazi uniforms and swastikas, would inflict psychological trauma on its large Jewish population, some of whom had lived through the Holocaust. The court of appeals acknowledged that "many people would find [the] demonstration extremely mentally and emotionally disturbing." Mentioning *Contreras*, the court also noted that Illinois recognizes the emerging tort of intentional infliction of severe emotional distress, which might well include racial slurs. Nevertheless, the threat of criminal penalties imposed by the ordinance impermissibly limited the plaintiffs' First Amendment rights.

Should our legal system offer redress for the harm of racist speech? The Washington case, from a liberal state court, implies that it should, at least if the remedy takes the form of a private action, a tort suit. *Phelps* and *Collins* (the Skokie case) imply that it should not, if the remedy takes the form of criminal punishment for behavior that took place in a public location.

A relatively recent cross-burning case, *Virginia v. Black*, suggests that punishment is constitutional if the hateful action takes place on private property and is targeted—aimed to intimidate a specific victim. Tort law, rooted in ancient Anglo-American tradition, has often served as a testing ground for new social sensibilities, which are later incorporated into our public law, for example campus conduct codes (see, e.g., chapter 2) or criminal statutes. Tort law thus serves as a kind of social laboratory for testing theories and assessing harms, which later can find their way into legislation and constitutional interpretation. Internet law may be the next such laboratory, as it is becoming increasingly clear that this is the site of some of the worst forms of social behavior (see chapter 3). As the reader will see, the cases in these two chapters span a long period and illustrate the slow development of the notion that society and its members require protection from hateful speech. Full citations to the main cases and principal texts can be found in an abbreviated list of references at the end of the book.

What, then, are some of the harms associated with racial insults? And how have courts viewed them over the years?

PSYCHOLOGICAL, SOCIOLOGICAL, AND POLITICAL EFFECTS OF RACISM

American society remains deeply afflicted by racism. Long before slavery became the mainstay of the plantation society of the antebellum South, Anglo-Saxon attitudes of racial superiority left their stamp on the developing culture of colonial America. Today, a century and a half after the abolition of slavery, many citizens suffer from discriminatory attitudes and practices infecting our economic system, cultural and political institutions, and the daily interactions of individuals. The idea that color is a badge of inferiority and a justification for the denial of opportunity and equal treatment is deeply ingrained.

Racial insults and remarks are among the most pervasive means by which discriminatory attitudes are imparted, communicating the message that distinctions of race are ones of merit, dignity, status, and personhood. Not only does the listener learn and internalize these messages, they color our institutions and are transmitted to succeeding generations.

The psychological harms of racial stigmatization are often much more severe than those created by other stereotyping actions, such as being left off a party list or being lined up, along with others like you, in the back row of the stage for a graduation exercise. Unlike many characteristics upon which stigmatization may be based, membership in a racial minority can be considered neither self-induced, like alcoholism or prostitution, nor alterable. Race-based stigmatization is therefore "one of the most fruitful causes of human misery. Poverty can be eliminated—but skin color cannot."

Minorities may come to believe frequent accusations that they are lazy, ignorant, dirty, and superstitious. It is neither unusual nor abnormal for stigmatized individuals to feel ambivalent about their self-worth and identity. This ambivalence arises from their awareness that others perceive them as falling short of societal standards, ones that even the individual may have internalized.

It is no surprise, then, that racial stigmatization injures its victims' relationships with others. Racial tags discourage interracial behavior and even that with members of one's own group.

The consequences of racism may also include mental illness and psychosomatic disease, including alcoholism, high blood pressure, and drug addiction. The rate of depression is considerably higher in minority communities than in society as a whole. Women who have fallen prey to Internet stalking, trolling, and "revenge porn" report similar distress, nightmares, and inability to function or work.

Achievement of high socioeconomic status does not reduce the risk of these harms. People of color who work and live in white-dominated settings, such as a law office or a bank, have more encounters with race and racism than ones living in a working-class black neighborhood, for example, and the effort to achieve success in business and managerial careers exacts a psychological toll even among exceptionally ambitious and upwardly mobile individuals. Those who succeed often do not enjoy the full benefits of their high status, resulting in stress and frustration.

Racial stigmatization may also affect parenting practices among minority group members. A study of minority mothers found that many denied the significance of color in their lives, yet were highly sensitive to it. Some overidentified with whites and white culture, including shopping habits, as though accepting whiteness as superior. It goes without saying that parents preoccupied with the ambiguity of their own social position are unlikely to raise confident, achievement-oriented, and emotionally stable children.

In addition to these psychological harms, racial abuse may have physical consequences, such as hypertension and strokes. The strong correlation between degree of darkness of skin and level of stress suggests that the greater discrimination experienced by darker-skinned minorities lies at the bottom of it. In addition to emotional and physical harms, racial stigmatization may damage a victim's wage-earning power. The person who is timid, withdrawn, bitter, hypertense, or psychotic is apt to fare poorly in job interviews. An experiment in which blacks and whites of similar aptitudes and capacities were put into a competitive situation found that blacks exhibited defeatism and made halfhearted efforts.

Racial labeling and racial insults harm the perpetrator as well by reinforcing rigid thinking and paranoia. Little evidence suggests that racial slurs serve as a "safety valve" for anxiety that would otherwise find expression in violence (see chapter 4).

Racism and racial stigmatization harm not only victims and perpetrators but society as a whole. They contravene the ideal of egalitarianism, that "all men are created equal" and each person is an equal moral agent, a value that is a cornerstone of the American moral and legal system. A society in which some members regularly are subjected to degradation because of their race hardly exemplifies this ideal. Moreover, unredressed breaches of this goal may demoralize onlookers who prefer to live in a truly equal society and don't like to see violations of this principle taking place regularly around them.

Of course, racism and racial labeling have an even greater impact on children than on adults. In a classic study, when presented with otherwise identical dolls, a black child preferred the light-skinned one as a friend; another said that the dark-skinned one looked dirty or "not nice." A third disliked her skin so intensely that she "vigorously lathered her arms and face with soap in an effort to wash away the dirt." When asked about making a little girl out of clay, a black child said that the group should use the white clay rather than the brown "because it will make a better girl." When asked to describe dolls that had the physical characteristics of black people, young children chose adjectives such as rough, funny, stupid, silly, smelly, stinky, or dirty. Three-fourths of a group of four-year-old black children favored white play companions; over half felt themselves inferior to whites. Some engaged in denial or falsification.

The Special Harms of Racial Insults

In addition to these harms associated with racism and racist treatment, certain specific harms result from racial insults and invective. Immediate mental or emotional distress is the most obvious direct harm. A racial insult is always a dignitary affront, a direct violation of the victim's right to be treated respectfully.

Most racial taunts are intentional, not inadvertent. There can be little doubt that the dignitary affront of racial put-downs, except perhaps ones that are merely overheard, is intentional and therefore most reprehensible. Most people today know that certain words or combinations of them are offensive and only calculated to wound.

In addition to immediate emotional distress, racial insults inflict long-term psychological damage upon the victim. Social scientists who have studied the effects of racism have found that speech that communicates low regard for an individual because of race inscribes disabling stereotypes and apathy in those constantly subjected to it.

This is especially so for children. If the majority defines them and their parents as inadequate, dirty, incompetent, and stupid, the child will find it difficult not to accept those judgments. Much of the blame for the formation of these attitudes lies squarely on value-laden words, epithets, and racial names.

The child who is the constant victim of belittlement can react with only two strategies, hostility or passivity. Aggressive reactions can lead to consequences that reinforce the harm caused by the insults: children who behave aggressively in school are marked by their teachers as troublemakers. Passive reactions, however, yield no better results: children who are passive toward their tormentors turn the aggressive response on themselves, leading to apathy and withdrawal into fantasy or fear.

The Need for a Legal Remedy

The various harms associated with racial treatment argue for some sort of social sanction. Indeed, courts are already affording relief, usually by smuggling in recovery under some conventional, already recognized legal theory such as defamation or the tort of intentional infliction of emotional distress.

The main question law reformers are asking is whether a new, *freestanding* remedy is in order. The case for one seems strong: we are already protecting the interest at stake, but calling it something else. Moreover, a direct remedy might do some good. As judge A. Leon Higginbotham, author of *In the Matter of Color*, put it: "For most people living in racist societies, racial prejudice is merely a special kind of convenient rationalization for rewarding behavior."

In other words, in racist societies most citizens will exhibit both prejudice and discrimination. When social pressures and rewards for racism are missing, bigotry is likely to be restricted to people for whom prejudice fills a psychological need. By contrast, in a tolerant setting, even prejudiced persons will often refrain from discriminating in order to escape social disapproval.

Because most citizens comply with legal rules, a tort action for racial insults would discourage harmful activity through the teaching function of the law. Establishing a legal norm against hate speech would certainly increase public consciousness of its harm. Then, the behavior of citizens toward each other would reflect the values of a mature society more consistently than it does now.

As mentioned, the law already does provide a degree of protection from racial insults under such legal theories as assault, battery, intentional infliction of emotional distress, defamation, and various statutory and constitutional causes of action. Following are a few examples:

Battery

In *Fisher v. Carrousel Motor Hotel, Inc.*, the plaintiff, an African American mathematician attending a NASA convention in Texas, was accosted by a white restaurant employee while waiting in a cafeteria line. The employee snatched an empty plate from the plaintiff's hand and told him in a loud voice that he could not eat in that cafeteria. The plaintiff did not allege that he was actually touched or that he feared physical injury, but rather that he was "highly embarrassed and hurt" by the employee's actions in the presence of his associates. But he did assert a battery based on the touching of his plate. The Texas Supreme Court affirmed his award, despite the minimal touching and lack of any physical harm.

Intentional Infliction of Emotional Distress

Courts on several occasions have upheld causes of action or verdicts for minority plaintiffs in cases that stemmed in large part from racial insults. Often, these cases proceed on a theory of battery, but others go forward under a theory of intentional infliction of emotional distress, a relatively new tort. In one, *Taylor v. Metzger* (1998), a superior officer referred to a black sheriff as "jungle bunny" in the course of a training exercise. A New Jersey court upheld his cause of action because "in this day and age," all supervisors should know better. Many other cases follow suit.

Defamation

Still others allege defamation, a civil action turning on harm to one's reputation. Often these are less successful, unless coupled with one of the categories mentioned above. In *Bradshaw v. Swagerty*, for example, the court noted that "[t]he term 'nigger' is one of insult, abuse and belittlement harking back to slavery days. Its use is resented, and rightly so." Nevertheless the court denied recovery since the insult did not fall into one of the categories (impugning a woman's chastity, calling a lawyer a shyster) recognized as slanderous per se. Tellingly, in at least three older cases, white plaintiffs were permitted to sue for defamation against defendants who falsely charged that they were black.

Constitutional and Legislative Provisions

Finally, victims of racial insults who have sued state officials under the federal Civil Rights Act (section 1983) have occasionally achieved favorable results. In *Harris v. Harvey*, for example, a black police officer sued a white judge for a "racially motivated campaign to discredit and damage" the officer and have him relieved of his job. As part of his campaign, the judge had referred to the officer as a "black bastard." In affirming the jury's award, the Seventh Circuit held that "such an intentional tort inspired by racial animus and perpetrated under color of state law constitutes a denial of equal protection." The court also ruled that the judge's use of the power and prestige of his office brought his acts under color of law even though they did not fall within the scope of his judicial duties.

Similarly, courts and administrative bodies have imposed duties on prison officials, police officers, and school boards to avoid racial language, and found for the complaining party when they breached these duties and expectations. For example, in *Haddix v. Port of Seattle*, a case brought under a state antidiscrimination statute against a government agency for four years of abusive treatment by a white foreman, the jury awarded the plaintiff $200,000. One juror explained: "We set the sum $200,000 as a statement that race discrimination is wrong, and that the port is a public corporation and should be in the forefront of fighting discrimination."

Not every administrative channel is equally protective of the minority point of view, however. In *Matal v. Tam* (the "Slants" case), the Supreme Court held that the federal patents and trademark office had no business restricting a musical band from trademarking its name with a word that was derogatory to most Asians.

Objections to a Broad Remedy for Racial Insults

Recognition of a tort for racial insults has thus been proceeding intermittently and piecemeal, under a variety of different theories. Often defense attorneys are successful in having the case dismissed because the defendant's action did not fit an existing legal category, or because measuring damages would be difficult. Many urge, as does the ACLU, that the plaintiff would be better advised to toughen his hide. Sometimes, judges deny relief because they fear a "flood of litigation" or a mountain of fraudulent claims.

Occasionally, a defense attorney or judge will raise the objection that recognizing civil recovery for racial hate speech and invective violates the First Amendment's free-speech clause. But these objections are neither frequent nor prominent in these cases, because they concern private, interpersonal conduct—torts, in other words—rather than state action. This issue does arise in connection with disputes over statues and monuments in public parks and places, as well as with campus hate-speech rules at public universities and hateful tirades and trolling on the Internet (see chapters 2 and 3).

These are our next subjects. Many of the factual issues of harm, stigma, psychological damage, and injury to dignity and public values are similar in the private and public contexts, however, so it is helpful to keep this common background in mind.

2

HATE SPEECH ON CAMPUS

Over the past several years, hundreds of university and college campuses have experienced racial unrest that is serious or graphic enough to be reported in the press. Often, this takes the form of minority students requesting safe spaces, ethnic studies departments and faculty, trigger warnings, and crackdowns on hate speech and microaggressions. Other times, it results in demands that the school acknowledge its slave history, remove names of slave owners from campus buildings, or banish statues of Confederate heroes from the quad. Quite often it takes the form of a call for a campus conduct code banning hate speech—or civil libertarian demands to eliminate one as a violation of academic freedom or the Constitution's protection of free speech.

Of all these, those that concern speech have been the most hotly contested. Debates over hate-speech and campus-conduct codes began in the early 1990s with minority students pressing for hate-speech codes and defenders of free speech taking the other side. Even though the latter group have prevailed in most of the court challenges, campuses continue to search for means to rein in language that demoralizes and distracts minorities, making it more difficult for them to get an education. Other demands, such as the removal of Confederate names and statues, have traced much the same course, sometimes with greater success.

The controversy shows few signs of abating or even advancing very much. In contrast to the progress of tort doctrine, reviewed in chapter 1, the debate about campus hate speech and racist expression shows little progress. Both sides of the controversy seem to encounter difficulties in speaking in terms and frameworks that the other side will even understand.

One reason is that people tend to frame the issue of campus hate-speech rules in radically different ways. On learning that a university has enacted rules that forbid certain forms of speech, require trigger warnings, or remove symbols of a racist past, some will frame the issue as a First Amendment problem: the rules limit speech, and the Constitution forbids doing that without a very good reason. If one takes this as one's starting point, several consequences follow. First, the burden shifts to the other side to show that the interest in protecting members of the campus community from racial injury is compelling enough to overcome the presumption in favor of free speech. Moreover, the free-speech advocates will argue there must be no less onerous way of accomplishing that objective. Also, if we have such rules, someone will have to administer them. Won't that then raise the risk that the enforcer will become a censor, imposing narrow-minded restraints on campus discussion? What about slippery slopes and line-drawing problems: if a campus restricts racist remarks on the quad, might the temptation arise to do the same with classroom speech or political satire in the campus newspaper?

Others, however, will frame the problem as one of protection of equality. They will ask whether an educational institution does not have the power to protect core values emanating from the Thirteenth (forbidding slavery) and Fourteenth (equal protection) Amendments to enact reasonable regulations aimed at ensuring equal personhood on campus. If one characterizes the issue *this* way, different consequences follow. Now, the defenders of offensive speech are required to show that the interest in safeguarding such speech is compelling enough to overcome the preference for equal personhood. Moreover, we will want to be sure that this interest is advanced in the way least damaging to equality.

One encounters, again, concerns about the decision-maker who will enforce the rules, but from the opposite direction: the enforcer of the regulation must be attuned to the nuances of insult and white supremacy at issue, for example by incorporating multiethnic representation into the hearing process or board. Finally, a different set of slopes will look slippery. If we do not intervene to protect equality here, what will the next outrage be? One's analysis thus leads to the opposite conclusions depending on the starting point.

But an even deeper indeterminacy looms. Both sides invoke different narratives to rally support for their position. Protectors of the First Amendment see campus anti-racism rules as parts of a much longer story: the centuries-old struggle of Western society to free itself from superstition and enforced ignorance. The tellers of this story invoke martyrs like Socrates, Galileo, and Peter Zenger, and heroes like Locke, Hobbes, Voltaire, and Hume who fought for the right of free expression. They conjure up struggles against official censorship, book burning, witch trials, and communist blacklists. Compared to that stirring account, the minority protector's interest in freeing a few (supersensitive?) individuals from momentary discomfort seems, well, a little thin. A textured, historical account is pitted against a particularized, slice-of-life, dignitary one.

But those on the minority-protection side invoke a different, but no less powerful, narrative. They see a nation's centuries-long struggle to free itself from racial and other forms of tyranny, including slavery, lynching, Jim Crow laws, and separate-but-equal schools. They conjure up different milestones— Lincoln's Emancipation Proclamation and *Brown v. Board of Education*; they look to different heroes—Martin Luther King Jr., the early abolitionists, Rosa Parks, and Cesar Chavez, civil rights heroes who put their lives on the line for racial justice. Arrayed against that richly textured historical account, the racist's interest in insulting a person of color face-to-face looks thin.

One often hears that the problem of campus anti-racism rules is that of balancing free speech and equality. But more is at issue. Each side wants not merely to have the balance struck in its favor; each wants to impose its own understanding of what is at stake. Minority spokespersons see the injury of one who has been subject to a racial assault as not a mere isolated event, but as part of an interrelated series of acts by which persons of color are subordinated, and are reinscribed with long histories of vilification that will follow them wherever they go. First Amendment defenders see the wrong of silencing the racist as much more than a momentary inconvenience: protection of his right to speak is part of the never-ending vigilance necessary to preserve freedom of expression in a society that is too prone to balance it away.

Both stories are equally valid. Judges and university administrators have no easy, a priori way of choosing, of privileging one over the other. They could coin an exception to free speech, thus giving primacy to the equal protection values at stake. Or, they could carve an exception to equality, saying in effect that universities and other social actors may protect minority populations except where this curtails speech. Nothing in constitutional or moral theory requires one answer rather than the other. Social science, case law, and the experience of other nations provide some illumination (see chapters 1 and 6). But ultimately, judges and university administrators must choose. And in making this choice, we are in uncharted terrain: we lack a polestar.

FRAMING THE ISSUE

Incidents of racism and other forms of bigotry have been spreading like wildfire on the nation's campuses. Some universities have done as little as possible or have focused on specific episodes or perpetrators, such as fraternities and other living groups. Others have instituted broad-based reforms, ranging from curricular changes to adoption of student conduct rules penalizing racist speech and acts. Some universities have taken action in the wake of a shocking incident, such as a cross burning on campus, a fraternity party featuring blackface or racist songs, or a noose hanging outside a building housing a black student organization. Some reforms went into place as preemptive measures, spurred by unrest at a sister school, which the authorities feared could spread to their campus. Occasionally, administrators took action spurred by angry responses to a conservative speaker or a posting or tweet by a faculty member that struck progressive students as racist. Other incidents arose in reaction to anonymous chalkings, graffiti, or email or Twitter postings.

Occasionally, controversy arises over a measure such as newly adopted speech codes that free-speech defenders or libertarians deemed excessive or wrongheaded. Universities should be "bastions of freedom," they assert. Hate-speech rules and other such measures run counter to the ideal of the university as a sanctuary of free thought.

These defenders see safe houses, trigger warnings, and hate-speech codes as throwbacks to the days when colleges and universities functioned *in loco parentis*, and wonder what might come next: rules attempting to regulate student sexuality or alcohol and drug consumption. Some see Big Brother and the rise of political correctness.

Many urge that more speech, not less, is the solution to offensive speech, so that convening a town hall or study group is the best approach. Indeed, incidents like these can be "teachable moments" enabling the various factions to come together and thresh out their differences. Others deplore what they see as coddling of minorities and women. In their view, speech is not the real problem. Minority students arrive at the university unprepared. As a result, they are unable to earn good grades, settle in, and defend themselves in campus debates.

Speech Codes

Today, over two hundred universities have enacted hate-speech or student-conduct codes forbidding hate speech of various kinds on campus. Although these codes are generally narrowly drafted, forbidding only the most reprehensible forms of speech and conduct, some have drawn the ire of free-speech organizations like FIRE (Foundation for Individual Rights in Education) and the ACLU. Not every college or university with such a code has been sued, but the ACLU's record is nearly perfect. In a number of highly publicized cases at major universities (including Stanford, Michigan, and Wisconsin), they succeeded in having the court strike down each one.

This has not stopped campus administrators, many of whom firmly believe that maintaining a healthy, supportive campus climate and atmosphere is essential to their mission. They believe, moreover, that the times demand such and are aware that many in the surrounding society—even some judges—share their view. They correctly note that the *social* norm against hate speech is now relatively well established, even if the *legal* version is not. Thirty years ago, it was possible to say, "What Jones said just now was hate speech, all right. What of it?" Today it is generally not (except perhaps during certain presidential campaigns).

Almost everyone condemns it—except the legal system.

This divergence, with society at large believing one thing and the legal system quite another, means that many conversations feature speakers talking past one another.

Most colleges and universities are strongly motivated to maintain an environment that is friendly to students of color, women, and sexual minorities. This stands to reason, for many campus administrators are committed to the goal of educating students for roles in a multicultural and multiracial world, and if the campus is cold or hostile, this goal will be difficult to achieve.

In short, the law in action—on university campuses, at least—is radically different from the law on the books. University presidents and administrators believe in one norm and the courts and ACLU in another. The administrators outnumber the judges and, until the Supreme Court issues a definitive ruling, are likely to continue to ignore lower court decisions in other jurisdictions in the belief that doing so is necessary to their mission. Some may believe that *Grutter v. Bollinger* (the affirmative action case) gives them the go-ahead to do so. *Grutter* held that universities may consider race in admissions in order to contribute to a tolerant multicultural society. They know, moreover, that minority students, like young women, are at a formative age in their development and may lack either the critical mass or self-confidence to defend themselves from a tide of microaggressions and put-downs.

Legal Realism

A few legal scholars and theorists support their position. These scholars note that legal realism, a progressive movement that swept the law in the early years of the past century and is now widely accepted, counsels that First Amendment doctrine needs to move beyond mechanical tests, such as no content regulation, and thought-ending clichés such as "the best cure to bad speech is more speech."

As with most areas of law, these theorists maintain, First Amendment controversies will benefit from empirical and multidisciplinary knowledge as well as consideration of the role of politics and social influence on judges, and the need to consider competing perspectives or models.

Legal realism paved the way for reform of many areas of the law, such as family law, contracts, and the law of corporations. It helped legal thought move beyond sterile doctrinal analysis that pretended that every legal question had one right answer. It enabled the law to respond more flexibly to the needs of a changing society and to gain from the perspectives of a host of companion disciplines, such as the social sciences or economics. But little of this found a home in First Amendment theory, with the result that American law in this area evokes wonder and consternation in the minds of thoughtful judges and scholars in the rest of the world (see chapter 6).

This frozen-in-time quality of American free-speech law is ironic, since the First Amendment is said to be a principal tool that our legal system uses to evaluate and facilitate change.

First Amendment Articles of Faith

The debate surrounding campus anti-racism rules has not only proceeded in an experiential vacuum, ignoring the example of other societies; it has also proceeded in a theoretical one, blind to the insights of social scientists who have studied race and racism. Critics of anti-racism rules, for example, often assert that (1) rules forbidding racist remarks will simply cause racism to go underground or surface in a more virulent form; (2) racist speech serves as a form of release, allowing prejudiced individuals to blow off steam harmlessly; (3) punishing racist speech is ineffective because it does not deal with the "root" causes of racism; and (4) the harm of a racial insult is *de minimis*. But these assertions are entirely unproven. Legal realism would counsel that they come in for serious examination, especially on college campuses, where the stakes are high. We are dealing, after all, with young minds and psyches and, therefore, the future of the country.

TWO DIFFERENT PERSPECTIVES

One reason why controversies over campus hate speech persist and never come to a resolution lies in the radically different perspectives that the two sets of protagonists take. Campus administrators generally favor restraints on hate speech and action, believing that they are necessary to maintaining a healthy diverse climate in which all can flourish.

Their approach, in short, is pragmatic and forward looking. They value speech and a robust exchange of views but believe that in order to maximize that value they must first ensure a variety of speakers and points of view, something that is unlikely to come about until they are able to provide a campus atmosphere in which all contributors feel welcome and safe.

Traditional First Amendment lawyers, by contrast, may approach the very same issues from a backward-looking perspective in which the dominant question is what we decided in this or that case fifty years ago, when society was less diverse than it is now. Those cases might be ones in which Nazis sought to march in Skokie, or a movie theater operator sought permission to show pornographic movies in a quiet, middle-class neighborhood. To the campus administrator merely trying to get things to simmer down in time for finals, all these matters may seem beside the point. To the legal scholar, they may be the whole point; for such a person, the

First Amendment must be a seamless web—and if one-quarter of the blacks and Latinos on a campus transfer to Howard or UC Riverside because of a torrent of hate messages or Confederate symbols, that is the price we pay for living in a free society.

One camp, in short, looks forward, the other back. Since overt racism was more acceptable in earlier times than it is today, the legal system is apt to have exhibited a higher toleration for it then than we believe is desirable now. Thus, the debate over forward- or backward-looking—"pragmatic" versus "principled"—perspectives and ways of reasoning is loaded and seems never to come to a happy end. Each side embeds a conclusion and a point of view in the very terms of the argument and the values and premises it considers relevant.

Moreover, as mentioned, each side invokes a different paradigm, with different heroes, myths, and notions of what is at stake in the argument. First Amendment absolutists talk about campus events using a different framework from that of the more pragmatic, policy-minded campus administrators who worry about keeping the peace and preserving the university's image.

A typical member of the free-speech faction is apt to cite heroic figures who stood up to narrow-minded orthodoxy and deploy metaphors such as the marketplace of ideas to rally the troops. The catchwords and maxims of such a person ("the best cure for bad speech is more speech"; "we must protect the speech we hate as much as, or more than, the speech we love"; hate speech as a pressure valve) tend to cluster together too, as do the lessons such a person draws from history ("free speech has been minorities' best friend; if they knew their own history, they would realize how unwise it is for them to be arguing for speech-restriction now").

Of course, the campus climate activist has a predictable parade of heroes and catchwords (implicit bias, microaggressions), metaphors (hate speech as silencing instrument), and maxims, too, for example, speech as violence. Each side deploys all these rhetorical tools against each other with varying degrees of certitude and impatience. The resulting intransigence that affects both sides naturally limits productive discussion: how can one reason with a maxim or a catchword?

The devices close down discussion, which often is their aim. How unsurprising then that the debate over campus climate never ends, or even advances much beyond a statement of the two initial positions. One has the law on its side, courtesy of

First Amendment formalism and a very slow rate of change; the other has (or believes it has) history, whose arc, it thinks, bends in its direction. By their very nature, these assertions are poorly calculated to help uncommitted listeners evaluate their merits.

In the meantime, minority students suffer and our national dialogue is impoverished.

3

HATE IN CYBERSPACE

The Internet is the site of some of the worst forms of racial and sexual vituperation. Perhaps the reason is that the usual social controls that moderate what we do in face-to-face encounters—normal inhibitions, conscience, religious teachings, disapproving looks of bystanders—do not operate, at least so effectively, in cyberspace. No one is looking over our shoulders. One operates, if one chooses, in complete anonymity; there is no easy way to trace one's identity. For this reason, the Internet, which includes email, Facebook, Twitter, blogs, Snapchat, Reddit, Instagram, Tinder, dating services, and much more, is rife with hateful statements of all kinds, including racism, white supremacy, trolling, misogyny, and anti-Muslim, anti-Semitic, and pro-Nazi remarks and messages.

None of these behaviors is entirely new; indeed, some were common before the Internet came into wide use in the mid-1990s. The new medium merely made them easier and less costly to perform. More people misbehave online than do in person; and others, seeing how easy it is to do, sometimes follow suit. Sometimes this coordination is intentional, as when opponents of a liberal sociology professor send hundreds of emails to her administration hoping to get her fired. Unlike oral remarks, which disappear once they are spoken, or graffiti, which will be erased or painted over eventually, much material posted on the Internet will remain there indefinitely, becoming a permanent part of the visible landscape. If a hate message "goes viral," millions of viewers may see it. This may be why many citizens are now, for the first time, beginning to realize how white-supremacist attitudes are shockingly commonplace.

The Internet, of course, does a lot of good. People can research subjects and find the answers to their questions. Friends separated by hundreds or thousands of miles can keep in touch. The police can inform citizens of crime in their neighborhoods. But as law professor Danielle Citron notes, the Internet is the Wild West: anything goes.

Unlike college campuses, which are somewhat susceptible to reasonable regulation, the Internet is, to this date, outside any form of governmental or state control—except in Europe and other foreign areas. The main sources of controls in the United States are peer pressure and any rules enacted by those who operate the sites and search engines, such as Facebook, Google, Bing, GoDaddy, and Yahoo. Talking back to the aggressor is often impossible, since one may not know who the aggressor is. And it is hard to toughen one's hide in response to a message that may have gone viral or that attracts the prurient curiosity of people in your neighborhood or social circle, such as a picture of you without clothes.

As Citron and others point out, private law, including tort suits for invasion of privacy, defamation, or intentional infliction of emotional distress, is a potential source of restraint, as is criminal law in certain extreme situations. Women victimized by "revenge porn" (photos of themselves distributed by jilted lovers) have succeeded in having the photos removed, and a few district attorneys have prosecuted malicious posters of damaging material that caused a victim's death or suicide. Unmasking the poster is possible in the course of civil or criminal discovery, although it is not easy.

What can we learn from this situation? One lesson is that human nature is not necessarily good, especially when it is easy and cost-free to misbehave. Another is that controls may actually work, but their absence leads to increased irresponsible behavior.

As more users, including worried parents, shrink from Internet use because of what they find there, advertisers, web page designers, and Silicon Valley may find new ways to control the worst forms of abuse and vituperation in this new and enticing theater of operation. Some are doing this now. As we went to press, Google, PayPal, GoDaddy, and Facebook were banishing a growing list of extremist groups and individuals for violating their terms of service. The Electronic Frontier Foundation was monitoring the situation, concerned about hate and anti-Semitism online but also worried that government censorship could expand into legitimate areas.

The many private law remedies, such as suits for intentional infliction of emotional distress, defamation, invasion of privacy, assault, and others discussed above, are potentially available for those targeted by malicious Internet messages. State legislators and Congress, under its power to regulate commerce, may eventually take action, as governments have done in many other countries. Until then, the Internet will continue to provide graphic evidence of the ability of words to wound.

Finally, just as in the Wild West, it is sometimes hard to know who wears the white hat and who the black. A growing list of right-wing groups, including fringe churches, have been suing the Southern Poverty Law Center for listing them on its website as hate groups. The conservative churches are hate groups, in the SPLC's estimation, because they condemn homosexuality as a sin and sometimes take action to make life hard for gay people. But the churches believe that the Bible cannot be in error. The result of this impasse is that two groups are labeling each other as hate groups, with the labeling the main evidence for the complaint of one. Before the Internet made the rapid dissemination of information possible, the two groups might easily not have known about each other.

4

NEOLIBERAL ARGUMENTS AGAINST HATE-SPEECH REGULATION

In the wake of three recent decisions, one by the U.S. Supreme Court dealing with punishment for hate crimes (*Wisconsin v. Mitchell*), two by the Canadian Supreme Court upholding limitations on hate speech and pornography (*Regina v. Keegstra* and *Regina v. Butler*), and a fourth by the U.S. Supreme Court permitting punishment for cross burning (*Virginia v. Black*), interest in campus anti-racism measures has revived. In the late 1980s, a number of U.S. campuses had responded to a wave of racist incidents by enacting student conduct codes forbidding certain types of racist expression. Then, federal courts struck down codes that were in effect at two midwestern universities. And a short time later, the Supreme Court invalidated a Saint Paul, Minnesota, hate-speech ordinance under which a white youth had been convicted of burning a cross on the lawn of a black neighbor (*R.A.V. v. St. Paul*). Many institutions that had been considering hate-speech rules put them on hold.

But the more recent decision upholding enhanced sentences for defendants convicted of racially motivated crimes, coupled with the above-mentioned Supreme Court decision approving punishment for cross burning, together with recent scholarship on tort-based solutions, has spurred renewed interest in hate-speech regulation. Today, many authorities believe that properly drafted prohibitions could now be put in place. But will they be?

Not without a fight. No longer certain that wooden, mechanistic First Amendment jurisprudence will hold sway, opponents of hate-speech rules are beginning to argue that even if they could be put in place, they should not be. In short, good policy argues against it. This chapter addresses one form that resistance takes, namely the deployment of paternalistic objections to regulatory responses. In this approach, opponents of hate-speech rules simply announce that equality and freedom are really not opposed. If minorities truly understood their situation, they would not be clamoring for hate-speech rules, but would instead embrace the civil libertarian/free-speech position. Often these objections issue from the moderate left, sometimes from libertarians. Many of them are paternalistic in nature, reasoning that the best interest of minorities, properly understood, militates against protecting them from hate speech.

Our decision to focus on these objections is sparked by more than mere theoretical interest. Respected writers and commentators, including the former national president of the ACLU, make such arguments. Audiences listen and nod agreement. Unless challenged, these arguments may have more effect than they deserve.

In order to understand the interplay of arguments raging in the hate-speech debate, it is necessary briefly to review the development of anti-racism rules. That history has both social and legal aspects. Beginning some time ago, many campuses began noticing a sharp rise in the number of incidents of hate-ridden speech directed at minorities, gays, lesbians, and others. Experts have been divided on the causes of the upsurge. A few argue that the increase is the result of better reporting or heightened sensitivity on the part of the minority community. Most, however, believe that the changes are real, noting that they are consistent with a sharp rise in attacks on foreigners, immigrants, and ethnic minorities occurring in many Western industrialized nations. This general rise, in turn, may be prompted by deteriorating economies and increased competition for jobs. It may reflect an increase in populations of color, due to immigration patterns and high birthrates. It may be related to the ending of the Cold War and competition between the two superpowers.

Whatever its cause, campus racism is of great concern to many educators and university officials. At the University of Wisconsin, for example, the number of black students dropped sharply in the wake of highly publicized incidents of racism. Faced with negative publicity and declining minority enrollments, some campuses established programs aimed at racial awareness. Others broadened their curriculum to include more multicultural offerings, events, and theme houses. Still others enacted hate-speech codes that prohibit slurs and disparaging remarks directed against persons on account of their ethnicity, religion, or sexual orientation. Sometimes these codes are patterned after existing torts or the fighting-words exception to the First Amendment. One at the University of Texas, for example, bars personalized insults that are severe enough to create a hostile environment that interferes with the ability to work or study on campus. Another, at the University of California, prohibits words or contacts that incite violence or prejudicial action based on any of a number of characteristics.

It was not long until these codes began to be challenged in court. In *Doe v. University of Michigan*, the university unsuccessfully defended a student conduct code that prohibited verbal or physical behavior that "stigmatizes or victimizes" any individual on the basis of various immutable and cultural characteristics, and that "[c]reates an intimidating, hostile or demeaning environment." Citing Supreme Court precedent that requires speech regulations to be clear and precise, the district court found Michigan's code fatally vague and overbroad. Two years later, in *UWM Post, Inc. v. Board of Regents*, a different federal court considered a University of Wisconsin rule that prohibited disruptive epithets directed against an individual because of his or her race, religion, or sexual orientation. The court invalidated the rule, finding the measure overly broad and ambiguous. The court refused to apply a balancing test that would weigh the social value of the speech against its harmful effect, and found the rule's similarity to Title VII workplace doctrine insufficient to satisfy constitutional requirements.

More recent decisions, however, have supported the efforts of authorities to take action against racist conduct. In *Wisconsin v. Mitchell*, a black man was convicted of aggravated battery for severely beating a white youth. Because the defendant selected the victim for his race, the defendant's sentence was increased by an additional two years under a Wisconsin penalty-enhancement statute. The U.S. Supreme Court affirmed, holding that motive, and more specifically racial hatred, can be considered in determining the sentence of a convicted defendant. The Court explained that while "abstract beliefs, however obnoxious" are protected under the First Amendment, they are not protected once those beliefs express themselves in commission of a *crime*.

In Canada, two recent decisions also upheld the power of the state to prohibit certain types of offensive expression when they cause societal harm. In *Regina v. Keegstra*, a teacher had described Jews in disparaging terms to his pupils and declared that the Holocaust did not take place. The Supreme Court of Canada upheld the national criminal code provision under which the defendant was charged. The court emphasized that this type of hate speech harms its victims and society as a whole, sufficiently so to justify criminalizing it. In *Regina v. Butler*, the Supreme Court of Canada reversed a trial court dismissal of criminal pornography charges, based on the social harm caused by the speech and the minimal impairment of legitimate speech that the prohibition presented. Both decisions are notable because Canada's legal and free-speech traditions are similar to those of the United States, and because the Canadian Charter protects speech in terms similar to those of its U.S. counterpart.

The recent scholarly interest in torts-based approaches provides a final development suggesting the feasibility of regulating hate speech. Several scholars advocate regulating hate speech through the torts of intentional infliction of emotional distress or group defamation (see chapter 1). These scholars observe that the law of tort can supply models for harm-based codes that would pass constitutional muster. They emphasize that tort law's historic role in redressing personal wrongs, its neutrality, and its relative freedom from constitutional restraints are powerful advantages for rules aimed at curbing hate speech.

At present, then, case law and scholarly commentary, although divided, suggest that carefully drafted hate-speech restrictions may comply with the First Amendment. The future thus seems to lie in the hands of policymakers.

FOUR PATERNALISTIC OBJECTIONS

Because of the seeming feasibility of drafting constitutional hate-speech regulations, the debate over such rules has shifted to the policy arena. Four arguments made by opponents of anti-racism rules are central to this debate:

- Permitting racists to utter racist remarks and insults allows them to blow off steam harmlessly. As a result, minorities are safer than they would be under a regime of anti-racism rules. We refer to this as the "pressure valve" argument.
- Anti-racism rules will end up hurting minorities, because authorities will invariably apply the rules against them rather than against members of the majority group. This we call the "reverse enforcement" argument.
- Free speech has been minorities' best friend. Because free speech is a principal instrument of social reform,

persons interested in achieving reform, such as minorities, should resist placing any fetters on freedom of expression if they know their self-interest. This we term the "best friend" objection.

- More speech—talking back to the aggressor—rather than regulation is the solution to racist speech. Because racism is a form of ignorance, dispelling it through reasoned argument is the only way to get at its root. Moreover, talking back to the aggressor is empowering. It strengthens one's own identity, reduces victimization, and instills pride in one's heritage. This we call the "talk back" argument.

Each of these arguments is paternalistic, invoking the interest of the group seeking protection. Each is seriously flawed; indeed, the situation is often the opposite of what its proponents understand it to be. Racist speech, far from serving as a pressure valve, deepens minorities' predicament. Moreover, except in authoritarian countries like South Africa, authorities generally do not apply anti-racism rules against minorities. Free speech has not always proven a trusty friend of racial reformers. Finally, talking back is rarely a realistic possibility for the victim of hate speech.

The Pressure Valve Argument

The pressure valve argument holds that rules prohibiting hate speech are unwise because they increase the danger racism poses to minorities. Forcing racists to bottle up their dislike of people of color means that they will be more likely to say or do something even more hurtful later. Free speech thus functions as a pressure valve, allowing tension to dissipate before it reaches a dangerous level. Pressure valve proponents argue that if minorities understood this, they would oppose anti-racism rules.

The argument is paternalistic; it says we are denying you what you say you want, and for your own good. The rules, which you think will help you, will really make matters worse. If you knew this, you would join us in opposing them.

But is this really so? Hate speech may make the speaker feel better, at least temporarily, but it does not make the victim safer. Quite the contrary, psychological evidence suggests that permitting one person to say or do hateful things to another increases, rather than decreases, the chance that he or she will do so again. Moreover, others may believe it is permissible to follow suit. Human beings are not mechanical objects. Our behavior is more complex than the laws of physics that describe pressure valves, tanks, and the behavior of a gas or liquid in a tube. In particular, we use symbols to construct our social world, a world that contains categories and expectations for "black," "woman," "child," "immigrant," "criminal," "wartime enemy," and so on. Once the roles we create for these categories are in place, they govern the way we speak of and act toward members of those categories in the future.

Even simple barnyard animals act on the basis of categories. Poultry farmers know that a chicken with a single speck of blood may be pecked to death by the others. With chickens, of course, the categories are neural and innate, functioning at a level more basic than language. But social science experiments demonstrate that the way we categorize others affects our treatment of them. An Iowa teacher's famous "blue eyes / brown eyes" experiment showed that even a one-day assignment of stigma can change behavior and school performance. At Stanford University, Philip Zimbardo assigned students to play the roles of prisoner and prison guard, but was forced to discontinue the experiment when some of the participants began taking their roles too seriously. At Yale University, Stanley Milgram showed that many members of a university community could be made to violate their conscience if an authority figure invited them to do so and assured them this was permissible and safe.

The evidence, then, suggests that allowing persons to stigmatize or revile others makes them more aggressive, not less. Once the speaker forms the category of deserved victim, his or her behavior may continue and escalate to bullying and physical violence. Further, the studies demonstrate that stereotypical treatment tends to generalize—what we do teaches others that they may do likewise. Pressure valves may be safer after letting off steam; human beings are not.

The Reverse Enforcement Argument

Others argue that enactment of hate-speech rules is sure to hurt minorities because the new rules will be applied against minorities themselves. A vicious insult hurled by a white person to a black will go unpunished, but even a mild expression of exasperation by a black motorist to a police officer or by a Latino student to a professor, for example, will bring harsh retribution. The argument is plausible because certain authorities are indeed racist and dislike minorities who speak out of turn, and because a few incidents of people of color charged with hate speech for innocuous behavior have occurred. The former president of the ACLU, for example, asserts that in Canada, shortly after the Supreme Court upheld a federal hate-speech code, prosecutors began charging blacks with hate offenses.

But the empirical evidence does not suggest that this is common, much less the rule. Police and FBI reports show that hate crimes are committed much more frequently by whites against blacks than the reverse. Statistics compiled by the National Institute Against Violence and Prejudice confirm what the police reports show, that a large number of minorities are victimized by racist acts on campus each year. Moreover, the distribution of enforcement seems to be consistent with commission of the offense. Although an occasional minority group member may be charged with a hate crime or with violating a campus hate-speech code, these prosecutions seem rare.

Racism, of course, is not a one-way street; some minorities have harassed and badgered whites. And a study showed that in repressive societies, such as South Africa and the former Soviet Union, laws against hate speech have indeed been deployed to stifle dissenters and members of minority groups. Yet this has not happened in more progressive countries. The likelihood that officials in the United States would turn hate-speech laws into weapons against minorities thus seems remote.

Free Speech as Minorities' Best Friend: The Need to Maintain the First Amendment Inviolate

Many absolutists urge that the First Amendment historically has been a great friend and ally of social reformers. They point out that without free speech, Martin Luther King Jr. could not have moved the American public as he did. Other reform movements also are said to have relied heavily on free speech. This argument, like the two earlier ones, is paternalistic. It is based on the supposed best interest of minorities; if they understood that interest, the argument goes, they would not demand regulations to bridle speech.

This approach ignores the history of the relationship between racial minorities and the First Amendment. In fact, minorities have made the greatest progress when they acted in *defiance* of the First Amendment. The original Constitution protected slavery in several of its provisions, and the First Amendment existed contemporaneously with slavery for nearly one hundred years. Free speech for slaves, women, and the propertyless was simply not a major concern for the drafters, who appear to have conceived the First Amendment mainly as protection for the kind of refined political, scientific, and artistic discourse they and their class enjoyed.

Later, of course, abolitionism and civil rights activism broke out. But examining the role of speech in reform movements shows that the relationship of the First Amendment to social advance is not so simple as some believe. In the civil rights movement of the 1960s, for example, Martin Luther King Jr. and others did use speeches and other symbolic acts to kindle America's conscience. But as often as not, they found the First Amendment did not protect them from arrest and conviction. Their speech was seen as too forceful, too disruptive. To be sure, their convictions would sometimes be reversed on appeal many years later. But the First Amendment, as then understood, served more as an obstacle than a friend.

An examination of the current landscape of First Amendment exceptions to protecting free speech bears out this observation. Our legal system has carved out or tolerated dozens of "exceptions" to the free-speech principle: conspiracy; libel; copyright; plagiarism; official secrets; misleading advertising; words of threat; disrespectful words uttered to a judge, teacher, or other authority figure; and many more. These exceptions—each responding to some interest of a powerful group—seem familiar and acceptable, as indeed perhaps they are. But a proposal for a new exception to protect eighteen-year-old black undergraduates immediately produces consternation: the First Amendment must be a seamless web.

It is we, however, who are caught in a web, the web of the familiar. The First Amendment seems to us useful and valuable. It reflects our interests and sense of the world. It allows us to make certain distinctions, tolerates certain exceptions, and functions in a particular way we assume will be equally valuable for others. But the history of the First Amendment, as well as the current landscape of doctrinal exceptions, shows that it is far more valuable to the majority than to the minority, more useful for confining change than for propelling it.

More Speech:
Talking Back to the Aggressor

Defenders of the First Amendment sometimes argue that minorities should learn to talk back to the aggressor. One prominent civil libertarian, for example, writes that conduct codes teach minorities to depend on whites for protection, while talking back clears the air, emphasizes self-reliance, and strengthens one's self-image as an active agent in charge of one's own destiny. The "talking back" approach draws force from the First Amendment more-speech principle according to which additional dialogue is always a preferred response to speech that is problematic for some reason. Some believe that it is good for minorities to learn to speak on their own behalf. Moreover, a minority who speaks out may be able to educate the speaker who has uttered a racially hurtful remark. Racism, at least in some cases, results from ignorance or fear. If a victim of racist hate speech takes the time to explain matters, he or she may alter the speaker's perception so that she will act more appropriately in the future.

How valid is this argument? Like many paternalistic arguments, it is offered without evidence, virtually as an article of faith. In the nature of paternalism, those who make the argument are in a position of authority, and therefore believe themselves able to make things so merely by asserting them. The social world is as they assert because it is their world: they created it that way.

In reality, those who hurl racial epithets do so because they feel they can get away with doing it. Often, their principal objective is to reassert and reinscribe that power. One who talks back is perceived as issuing a direct challenge to that power. The action is seen as outrageous, calling for a forceful response. Often racist remarks are delivered in several-on-one situations, in which responding in kind is foolhardy. Indeed, many cases of racial homicide began in just this fashion. A group began badgering a black person. The person talked back, and paid with his life. Other racist remarks are delivered in a cowardly fashion, by means of graffiti scrawled on a campus wall late at night or on a poster placed outside of a black student's dormitory door. In these situations, more speech, of course, is impossible.

Racist speech is rarely a mistake, something that could be corrected or countered by discussion. After all, what would be the answer to "Nigger, go back to Africa. You don't belong at the university"? "Sir, you misconceive the situation. Prevailing ethics and constitutional interpretation hold that I, an African American, am an individual of equal dignity and entitled to attend this university in the same manner as others. Now that I have informed you of this, I am sure you will modify your remarks in the future"?

The idea that talking back is safe for the victim or educative for the racist simply does not correspond with reality. It ignores the power dimension to racist remarks, forces minorities to run very real risks, and treats a hateful attempt to force the victim outside the human community as an invitation for discussion. Even when successful, talking back is a burden. Why should minority undergraduates, already charged with their own education, be responsible for educating others?

CAMPUS ANTI-RACISM RULES
AND THEIR CHALLENGES

In the wake of recent court decisions, the task of drafting such rules is technically quite feasible. Consider two simple ways this could happen. Campus rules could be drafted either to prohibit expressions of racial hatred and contempt directly through a two-step approach, or to regulate behavior currently actionable in tort. In either case, the rules must be neutral and apply across the board, that is, must not single out particular forms of hateful speech for punishment while leaving others untouched. Moreover, any campus considering enacting such rules should be certain to compile adequate evidence of their necessity.

The direct approach would couple two provisions. The first would prohibit face-to-face invective calculated seriously to disrupt the victim's ability to function in a campus setting. This provision, which must be race-neutral, could be tailored to capture the content of any recognized First Amendment exception, such as fighting words or workplace harassment. Because of the university's special role and responsibility for the safety and morale of students, even the precaution of working within a recognized exception might not be necessary.

A second provision would provide enhanced punishment for any campus offense (including the one just described) which was proven to have been committed with a racial motivation. Such a two-step approach would satisfy all current constitutional requirements. It would promote a compelling and legitimate institutional interest. It would not single out particular types of expression, but rather particular types of motivation at the punishment stage. And it would not abridge rules against content or viewpoint neutrality, since it focuses not on the speaker's message but on its intended effect on the hearer, namely to impair his or her ability to function on campus.

Alternatively, a hate-speech rule could be patterned after an existing tort, such as intentional infliction of emotional distress or group libel, with the race of the victim a "special factor" calling for increased protection, as current rules and the Restatement of Torts (a recognized guidepost) already provide. Tort law's neutrality and presumptive constitutionality strongly suggest that such an approach would be valid. Harm-based rationales for punishing hate speech should be valid whenever the social injury from the speech outweighs its benefits.

The strongest reason for enacting hate-speech rules on campuses with a history of disruption is that they are necessary to promote equality. But even putting this aside and viewing the question purely through the free-speech lens, the policy concerns underlying our system of free expression are largely absent with hate speech. Targeted racist vitriol scarcely advances self-government or the search for consensus. It does not promote the search for truth, nor help the speaker reach self-actualization, at least in any ideal sense. Racist speech thus does little to advance any of the theoretical rationales scholars and judges have advanced as reasons for protecting speech.

Looking at the hate-speech problem from the perspective of enforcement yields no greater support for scathing speech. Our system distrusts any form of official speech regulation because we fear that the government will use the power to insulate itself from criticism. This danger is absent, however, when the government sets out to regulate speech between private speakers, especially about subjects falling outside the realm of politics. When the government intervenes to tell one class of speakers to avoid saying hurtful things to another, governmental aggrandizement is at best a remote concern. This is the reason why regulation of private speech—libel, copyright, plagiarism, deceptive advertising, and so on—rarely presents serious constitutional problems. The same should be true of hate speech.

Another political process concern is also absent. Our legal system resists speech regulation in part because of concern over selective regulation or enforcement. If the state received the power to declare particular speakers disfavored, it could effectively exclude them from public discourse. We would forfeit the benefit of their ideas, while they would lose access to an important means for advancing their own interest. But none of these dangers is present with hate speech. Allowing the government to create a special offense for a class of persons (even racists) is indeed troublesome, as the Supreme Court recognized in the first cross-burning case (*R.A.V. v. St. Paul*). But the direct approach we have outlined introduces the racial element only at the sentencing stage, where the dangers and political-process concerns of selective treatment are greatly reduced. The same would be true if the tort approach were adopted. In tort law, it is the intent and injury that matter, not the content of the speech. Enforcement comes from private initiative, not state action. Prevention of harm is the goal, with no speech disfavored as such. But will it happen?

In light of recent cases, there is little reason today in First Amendment jurisprudence for leaving campus hate speech unregulated. Censorship and governmental nest feathering are not serious problems when authorities seek to regulate speech between private citizens. Nor does racial vilification promote any of the theoretical rationales for protecting free speech. Far from acting as a pressure valve that enables rage to dissipate harmlessly, epithets make matters worse. Pernicious images create a world in which some come to see others as proper victims. Like farmyard chickens with a speck of blood, they may be reviled, mistreated, denied jobs, slighted, spoken of derisively, even beaten at will.

The Greeks used the term *hubris* to describe the sin of believing that one may "treat[ ] other people just as one pleases, with the arrogant confidence that one will escape any penalty for violating their rights." Those who tell ethnic jokes and hurl racial epithets are guilty of this kind of arrogance. But some who defend these practices, including First Amendment purists, are guilty of it as well. Insisting on free speech over all, as though *no* countervailing interests were at stake, and putting forward transparently paternalistic justifications for a regime in which hate speech flows freely is also hubristic.

Some words, we have argued, have little purpose other than to subordinate, injure, and wound. Tinged with more than a little hubris, the liberals' paternalistic arguments do not hold. What about those of the conservatives?

5

NEOCONSERVATIVE ARGUMENTS AGAINST HATE-SPEECH REGULATION

Now it is time to consider neoconservatives and what we term the politics of denial.

As we noted earlier, the structure of the hate-speech debate has been undergoing a slow but inexorable shift. As First Amendment formalism, with its mechanistic doctrines, models, and tests, has begun giving way to First Amendment realism, both the moderate left and the moderate right, who much preferred things the old way, have changed their ground. Realizing, perhaps, that mechanical jurisprudence and case law laid down in an earlier era will not hold up much longer, they have been urging that even if First Amendment doctrine were to permit regulating hate speech, wisdom and good policy counsel against it.

A number of arguments characterize what we call the "toughlove" or neoconservative position:

- Pressing for hate-speech regulation is a waste of time and resources.

- White society will never tolerate speech codes, so that the effort to pass them is quixotic, symbolic, or disingenuous.
- Racist expression is a useful bellwether that should not be driven underground.
- Encouraging minorities to focus on slights and insults merely induces them to see themselves as victims.
- The campaign is classist, since it singles out the transgressions of the blue-collar racist while leaving the more genteel versions of the upper classes untouched.
- And the cure is worse than the disease, because it institutionalizes censorship, and "two wrongs don't make a right."

We call these arguments the "deflection," "quixotic," "bellwether," "victimization," "classist," and "two wrongs" arguments. What unites them are two themes. The first is that struggling against hate speech is a digression ("the real problem is . . ."), and the second is that the effort reinforces the idea of oneself as a victim, rather than an active agent in charge of one's destiny.

Let us consider the arguments in turn. As we shall see, neoconservatives take the positions they do on the hate-speech controversy because vituper-

ative speech aimed at minorities forces them to con-
front the intuition that slurs directed against people
of color are simply more serious than ones directed
against whites. This intuition, in turn, threatens a
prime conservative tenet, the level playing field. We
explain why the First Amendment version of that
field—namely, the marketplace of ideas—is not
at all level but slanted against people of color and
other minorities, and why talking back to the aggressor is rarely a satisfactory option for the victim.

THE DEFLECTION OR
WASTE-OF-TIME ARGUMENT

Many neoconservative writers argue that mobilizing against hate speech is a waste of precious time
and resources. One, a law school dean, writes that
civil rights activists ought to have better things to do,
and that concentrating on hate-speech reform is calculated to benefit only a small number of privileged,
upper-class minorities. Instead of "picking relatively
small fights of their own convenience," racial reformers
should be examining the obstacles that truly impede
racial progress, namely bad laws and too little money.

Others echo these remarks. Dinesh D'Souza, for
example writes that campus radicals espouse hate-

speech regulation because it is easier than study-ing hard and getting a first-rate education. Henry Louis Gates, in a cover story in the *New Republic*, writes that addressing racist speech does lip service to civil rights without dealing with the material re-ality of economic subordination.

But is it so clear that efforts to control hate speech are a waste of time and resources, at least compared to other problems that the activists could be addressing? What neoconservative writers ig-nore is that eliminating hate speech goes hand in hand with reducing what they consider "real rac-ism." Certainly, being the victim of hate speech is a less serious affront than being thrown out of one's house or job. It is, however, equally true that a so-ciety that speaks and thinks of minorities derisively is fostering an environment in which such dis-crimination will occur frequently. Hate speech, in combination with a panoply of media imagery, con-structs a picture of minorities in the public mind. This picture or stereotype varies from era to era but is rarely positive, including traits such as happy and carefree, lascivious, criminal, devious, treacherous, untrustworthy, immoral, and of lower intelligence.

This stereotype guides action, including motor-ists who fail to stop to aid a stranded black driver, police officers who hassle African American youths innocently walking on the streets, or landlords who act on hunches or unarticulated feelings in renting an apartment to a white over an equally or more qualified black or Mexican.

Even when they do not lead to consequences like these, racial barbs are painful. A white motorist who suffers an epithet ("goddam college kid!") may be momentarily stunned. But the epithet does not call upon an entire cultural legacy the way a racial epithet does, nor deny the victim's standing and personhood.

A further reason why neoconservatives ought to pause before throwing their weight against hate-speech regulation has to do with the nature of contemporary racism. Most neoconservatives, like many white people today, think that acts of out-and-out discrimination are rare. The racism that remains, they believe, is subtle or institutional. It lies in the arena of unarticulated feelings, practices, and patterns of behavior (like promotions policy at work) on the part of institutions. A forthright focus on speech and language may be one of the few means of addressing and curing this kind of racism. Thought and language are inextricably connected. A speaker asked to reconsider his or her use of language may begin to reflect on the way he or she thinks about a subject.

Words offer a window into our unconscious. Our choice of word, metaphor, or image gives signs of the attitudes we have about a person or subject. No readier or more effective tool offers itself than a focus on language to deal with subtle or latter-day racism. Since some neoconservatives are among the prime proponents of the notion that this form of racism is the only or the main one that remains, they should think carefully before taking a stand in opposition to measures that might make inroads into it. Of course, speech codes would not reach every form of demeaning speech or depiction. But a tool's unsuitability to redress every aspect of a problem is surely no reason for refusing to employ it where it is effective.

THE QUIXOTIC ARGUMENT

Neoconservatives also argue against hate-speech regulation on the ground that the effort is doomed or quixotic. White people will never accede to such rules. Proponents of hate-speech regulation surely must know this, hence their objectives are probably symbolic, tactical, or at any rate something other than what they say. Donald Lively, for example, writes that the U.S. Supreme Court has consistently rejected laws regulating speech, finding them vague and overbroad. He also writes that the anti-hate-speech campaign lacks vision and a sense of marketability—it simply cannot be sold to the American public. Henry Louis Gates demands to know how hate-speech activists can possibly believe that campus regulations will do much good even if enacted. If campuses are the seething arenas of racism that activists believe, how will campus administrators and hearing officials provide nondiscriminatory hearings on charges brought under the codes?

But is the effort to curb hate speech doomed or misguided? It might be seen this way if the gains to be reaped were potentially only slight. But, as we argued earlier, they are large; indeed our entire panoply of civil rights laws and rules depends for its efficacy on controlling the background of harmful depiction against which the rules and practices operate. In a society where minorities are thought and spoken of respectfully, few acts of out-and-out discrimination would take place. In one that harries and demeans them at every turn, even a determined judiciary will not be able to enforce equality and racial justice.

Moreover, success is more possible than toughlove adherents would like to acknowledge. A host of Western industrialized democracies have instituted laws against hate speech and hate crime, often in the face of initial resistance (see chapter 6). Some, like Canada, Great Britain, and Sweden, have traditions of respect for free speech and inquiry rivaling ours. Determined advocacy might well accomplish the same here. In recent years, several hundred college campuses have seen fit to institute student conduct codes penalizing face-to-face insults of an ethnic or similar nature, in order to advance interests that they considered central to their function, such as protecting diversity or providing an environment conducive to education.

In addition, powerful actors like government agencies, the writers' lobby, industries, and so on have generally been quite successful at coining free-speech exceptions to suit their interest—exceptions like libel laws, defamation, false advertising, copyright, plagiarism, words of threat, and words of monopoly, just to name a few. Each of these seems natural and justified—because time-honored—and perhaps each is. But the magnitude of the interest underlying these exceptions seems no less than that of a young black undergraduate subject to hateful abuse while walking late at night on campus. New regulation is of course subject to searching scrutiny in our laissez-faire age. But the history of free-speech doctrine, especially the landscape of exceptions, shows that need and policy have a way of being translated into law. The same may happen with hate speech.

THE BELLWETHER ARGUMENT

A further argument one hears from the anti-rule camp is that hate speech should not be driven underground, but allowed to remain out in the open. The racist whom one does not know, they say, is far more dangerous than the racist whom one does. Moreover, on a college campus, incidents of overt racism or sexism can serve as useful spurs for discussion and institutional self-examination. Yale Law Professor Stephen Carter, for example, writes that regulating racist speech will leave minorities no better off than they are now, while screening out "hard truths about the way many white people look at . . . us." D'Souza echoes this argument, but with a reverse twist, when he points out that hate-speech crusaders are missing a valuable opportunity. When racist graffiti or hateful fraternity parties proliferate, minorities should reflect on the possibility that this may signal something basically wrong with affirmative action. Instead of tinkering futilely with the outward signs of malaise, we ought to deal directly with the problem itself. A law review editor argues that anti-racism rules are tantamount to "[s]weeping the problem under the rug," whereas "[k]eeping the problem in the public spotlight . . . enables members [of the university community] to attack it when it surfaces."

How should we see this argument? In one respect, it does make a valid point. All other things being equal, the racist who is known is less dangerous than the one who is not. But the argument ignores a third alternative, namely the racist who is cured, or at least deterred by firm rules, policies, and expectations so as no longer to behave as he or she once did. Since most conservatives believe that rules and penalties change conduct (and are indeed among the strongest proponents of heavy penalties for crime), they should take seriously the possibility that campus guidelines against hate speech and assault would decrease those behaviors.

THE VICTIMIZATION ARGUMENT: DO HATE-SPEECH RULES ENCOURAGE PASSIVE, DEPENDENT BEHAVIOR?

A fourth argument many neoconservative critics of hate-speech regulations make is that prohibitions against verbal abuse are unwise because they encourage minorities to see themselves as victims. Instead of rushing to the authorities every time they hear something that wounds their feelings, minorities ought to learn to speak back or ignore the offending behavior. A system of rules and complaints reinforces in their minds that they are weak and in need of protection, that their lot in life is to be victimized rather than to make use of those opportunities that are available to them. Carter, for example, writes that anti-hate-speech rules cater to "those whose backgrounds of oppression make them especially sensitive to the threatening nuances that lurk behind racist sentiment." Lively warns that the rules reinforce a system of "supplication and self-abasement"; D'Souza, that they distort and prevent interracial friendships and encourage a crybaby attitude; Gates, that they reinforce a therapeutic mentality and an unhealthy preoccupation with feelings.

Would putting into place hate-speech rules encourage passivity and a victim mentality among minority populations? In most cases, no, for other alternatives will remain available as before. No African American or lesbian student is required to make a complaint when targeted by verbal abuse or invective. He or she can talk back or ignore it if he or she sees fit. Hate-speech rules simply provide an additional avenue of recourse to those who wish to take advantage of them. Indeed, one could argue that filing a complaint constitutes one way of taking charge of one's destiny—one is active, instead of passively "lumping it" when verbal abuse strikes.

It is worth noting that we do not make the victimization charge in connection with other offenses that we suffer, such as having a car stolen or a house burglarized, nor do we encourage those victimized in this manner to "rise above it" or talk back to their victimizers. If we see recourse differently in the two sets of situations, it may be because we privately believe that a black who is called "nigger" by a group of whites is in reality not a victim. If so, it would make sense to encourage him not to dwell on or sulk over the event. But this is different from saying that filing a complaint deepens victimization; moreover, many studies have shown it simply is untrue. Racist speech is the harm. Filing a complaint is not. No empirical evidence suggests that filing a civil rights complaint causes one to feel worse about oneself.

THE CLASSIST ARGUMENT

Others in the neoconservative camp dismiss the effort to limit hate speech through enactment of campus rules as classist. The rules will end up punishing only what naïve or blue-collar students do and say. The more refined, indirect, but more devastating expressions of contempt of the more highly educated classes will pass unpunished. Henry Louis Gates offers the following comparison:

(A) LeVon, if you find yourself struggling in your classes here, you should realize it isn't your fault. It's simply that you're the beneficiary of a disruptive policy of affirmative action that places underqualified, underprepared and often undertalented black students in demanding educational environments like this one. The policy's egalitarian aims may be well-intentioned, but given . . . that aptitude tests place African Americans almost a full standard deviation below the mean, even controlling for socioeconomic disparities, they are also profoundly misguided. The truth is, you probably don't belong here, and your college experience will be a long downhill slide.

(B) Out of my face, jungle bunny.

Lively and D'Souza make versions of the same argument.

In one respect, the classism argument is plainly off target. If, in fact, the prep school product is less likely to utter harsh words of this kind, or to utter only intellectualized versions like the one in Gates's case A, this may be because he is less racist in a raw sense. If, as many social scientists believe, prejudice tends to be inversely correlated with educational level, the wealthy and well educated may well violate hate-speech rules less often than others. And in any event, "Out of my face, jungle bunny" (Gates's case B) is a more serious example of hate speech because it is not open to argument or a more-speech response, and has overtones of a direct physical threat. The other version, while deplorable, is unlikely to be coupled with a physical threat, and is answerable by more speech. ("That's wrong. Not all of us are on a downward slide. My friend Jamila made the dean's list last semester.")

THE TWO WRONGS ARGUMENT

The "two wrongs" argument, which holds that hate speech may be wrong but prohibition is not the way to deal with it, is one of the relatively few arguments that both the moderate right and the moderate left put forward, although they do so in slightly different forms and for different reasons. The moderate left opposes hate-speech restrictions in part because although it detests racism, it loves free speech even more. For their part, neoconservatives oppose regulation because it is government, in most cases, that would be doing the regulating, and especially because in the area of speech, governing to them is synonymous with censorship.

Gates, for example, writes that "there is also a practical reason to worry about the impoverishment of the national discourse on free speech. If we keep losing the arguments, then we may slowly lose the liberties that they were meant to defend." He also warns that two wrongs don't make a right and laments that our society and legal system have fallen away from the classical ideal of civil rights and civil liberties as perfectly compatible goods for all. Lively writes that history teaches that campaigns to limit speech always end up backfiring against minorities because free speech is a vital civic good and even more essential for them than others. Virtually all the authors of the moderate right persuasion (and some of the moderate left as well) cite the fear of censorship or governmental aggrandizement. If we allow an arm of the state to decide what is harmful speech, soon little of the right of speech will survive.

By way of response, we note that the term "censorship" is appropriately attached to measures allowing the heavy hand of government to fall on weaker, unpopular private speakers, or else on political dissidents who are attempting to criticize or change government itself. With hate-speech regulation, however, few of the concerns that underlie our aversion to censorship are present. Hate speakers are criticizing not government, but someone weaker than themselves. In prohibiting it, universities are not attempting to insulate themselves from criticism; concerns over governmental self-perpetuation are absent. Similarly, the speech being punished is far from the core of political expression—it carries few ideas at all except "I hate and reject your personhood." Hate speech, in fact, silences the victim and drives him away from places where conversation is occurring. Thus, when the government regulates hate speech, it enhances and adds to potential social dialogue, rather than subtracts from it.

◆ ◆ ◆

Why do toughlove proponents embrace arguments like these? We believe the reason has to do with the way hate speech casts doubt on a principal tenet of the conservative faith: the level playing field. In First Amendment theory, the name of that playing field is the marketplace of ideas, in which messages and communications of all sorts supposedly vie on equal terms to establish themselves. Out of that engagement, at least in theory, truth—the best idea of all—will emerge.

The core difficulty that hate speech poses for the conservative mind is, simply, that there is no correlate—no analog—for hate speech directed toward whites. Nor is there any countering message that could cancel out the harm of "Nigger, you don't belong on this campus—go back to Africa."

Vituperation aimed at underdogs wounds; there is nothing comparably damaging that whites have to undergo. The word "honky" is more a badge of respect than a put-down. "Cracker," although disrespectful, still implies power, as does "redneck." The fact is that terms like "nigger," "spic," "faggot," and "kike" evoke and reinforce entire cultural histories of oppression and subordination. They remind the target that his or her group has always been and remains unequal in status to the majority group. Even the most highly educated, professional-class African American or Latino knows that he or she is vulnerable to the slur, the muttered expression, the fishy glance on boarding the bus, knows that his graduate degree, his accomplishments, his well-tailored suit are no armor against mistreatment at the hands of the least-educated bigot.

Hate speech, then, wounds in a way that finds no analog with respect to whites; nor is there any effective way for a victim to speak back or counter it, even when it is physically safe to do so. Even worse, the most frequently targeted groups evoke little sympathy from society or the legal system when they ask for protection. Society instead asks, why don't you just talk back? In other settings, the combination of the three features just named would cause us to conclude that the playing field is not level, but sharply slanted. Imagine, for example, an athletic competition in which one side is denied a powerful weapon (say, the forward pass) and the other side is permitted to deploy this weapon freely, because the rules prevent the first from doing anything to counter it when it is used (such as knocking down the ball); and changes in the rules are not permitted because this is said to violate the charter that established the game in the first place.

Surely, we would say that such a competition is rigged. Yet, something like that characterizes the predicament of minority victims of hate speech. Conservatives cannot allow themselves to see this, however, since it goes against some of their most basic assumptions, including free competition and merit.

The problem of hate speech will not go away by merely insisting on ideologically based truths that "must be so," nor by suggesting responses that ought to work, much less by blaming the victim or telling him that the problem is all in his head. Hate speech renders campuses uncomfortable and threatening to substantial numbers of students at vulnerable points in their lives. It helps construct and maintain a social reality in which some are constantly one-down. And it tolerates and creates a culture at odds with our deepest national values and commitments.

Coming to grips with hate speech does pose serious problems for a society committed both to equality and to individual freedom and autonomy. But resorting to facile arguments like those discussed in this chapter does little to advance the discussion. Neoconservatives should allow themselves to see what everyone else does—that hateful remarks and invective are a virulent form of inequality reinforcement—and join the serious search now gaining force for cures for this national disease.

6

HOW DO OTHER NATIONS HANDLE THIS PROBLEM?

To this point, we have argued that hate speech of all kinds is socially pernicious, with few redeeming features. We have also shown that legal realism—the emerging conception of the First Amendment—allows regulation, and that no policy argument stands in the way of it. Sometimes, however, one hears vague references to other societies that have prohibited racist or sexist hate speech, with ill effects.

It is possible to examine these claims. Not long ago, ARTICLE 19, a London-based international organization devoted to freedom of expression and the press, held a three-day conference at Essex University. Distinguished lawyers, activists, and diplomats from several dozen countries discussed the question of hate speech under domestic and international law. The conference papers appeared a year later under the title *Striking a Balance*. Edited by American attorney Sandra Coliver, the book features major figures in the international human rights community, delegates from European and Third World nations, and legal scholars from the United States and elsewhere.

Overviews by prominent authors note that the United States stands virtually alone in extending freedom of expression to what has come to be called hate speech. Most countries tolerate some degree of regulation. One author reminds readers that "[t]here is a communal as well as an individual dimension to human rights and freedoms," and that "the individual's right to promote racist views must . . . be defended [not only] in terms of individual rights, but in terms of the communal interests in equality." He urges that any sensible society would limit speech when it begins to endanger these interests.

A section of more than twenty-five "country reports" substantiates these generalizations and shows that European and Asian countries generally pay little attention to arguments such as the clichéd "pressure valve" argument (see chapter 4) or the notion that suppressing hate speech will just cause it to go underground (see chapter 5). They reject the idea that laws punishing hate speech are likely to be used against minorities, and consider that hate speech harms both individuals and society.

Few believe that punishing hate speech is apt to lead to censorship or thought control, while most consider that curbing hate speech is an essential tool for reducing ethnic hostilities and conflict.

The responses nevertheless vary. India, for example, has both a strong commitment to democracy and a recent history of bitter ethnic and religious conflict. No surprise that such a society would take strong action to discourage racist speech and restore the fragile interpretive community that is part of its democratic heritage and ideals; indeed, this is what it has done.

A country like the former Soviet Union, by contrast, is marked by balkanization and a tradition of centralized repressive government. Such a society would not likely rely on shared expression, dialogue, and other forms of communication to bind itself together. Rather, centralized authority serves that purpose. When intergroup conflict breaks out, the impulse to restore a communicative paradigm will be weak. Consequently, laws against hate speech will not be in force. If they are, they are apt to be used eccentrically, as in the case of dissidents.

There thus seems to be no single balance that will work for all cultures, or even for the same culture at different times. The appropriate balance between equality and freedom of expression may be a complex, shifting matrix that includes several different values. These include the ideal of community historically and aspirationally; the value placed on equality among the various national groups; the perception that minority populations are unfairly excluded or stigmatized; the degree to which speech is considered an important individual prerogative rather than a means of achieving community; and finally, the perception that minority groups lack the means to assert and defend themselves against vilification.

A slight change in the strength of any of these components in a given setting may cause the balance and attitudes toward hate-speech regulation to shift. For example, many universities in the United States and elsewhere have witnessed an increase in the number of students of color and women coupled with increased competition for slots and scholarships. If racist speech and action break out on such a campus, the institution is likely to turn to speech regulation to preserve or restore peace and community, just as countries do.

Liberty, including free speech, and community exist in a reciprocally dependent tension. Each presupposes the other. As defenders of hate-speech regulation argue, dialogue is fruitless without something approaching equality among the speakers. Free-speech advocates point out, with equal justification, that free speech is an important instrument for achieving social justice—equality presupposes liberty. Either value may be used rhetorically, or in the real world, to suppress the other. The demand for community may lead to conformity, censorship, and groupthink. Speech, if misused, can be used concertedly to oppress minority groups and coarsen society.

Perhaps the most valuable lesson to be gleaned from a review of transnational experiences with regulation and hate speech is that there are no simple answers. But one thing does seem clear. The experience of other countries shows that adopting hate-speech rules would not cause the sky to fall. America would be even more American.

7

A GUIDE FOR ACTIVIST
LAWYERS AND JUDGES

Up to this point, we have argued that hate speech harms its victims; that nothing in the emerging realist view of the First Amendment prevents society from taking steps to control that harm; and that good social policy does not stand in the way, either. Yet some judges and many progressive lawyers have been slower than others—particularly legal scholars and civil rights activists—in accepting the need for reform. In this chapter we offer a sympathetic treatment of the judges' dilemma. We also show how a kind of romantic totalism afflicts some lawyers, journalists, and First Amendment absolutists, causing them to prefer defending Nazis to defending their victims—the minorities who suffer from racist speech and invective.

As mentioned earlier, the debate about hate speech features two camps, each of which views the controversy in quite different terms (see chapter 2). One group, on learning about a proposed hate-speech rule or tort remedy, immediately declares the proposal a free-speech question. If one does this, a number of things immediately follow. The civil rights advocates are immediately placed on the defensive, seen as aggressors attempting to curtail a precious liberty. The burden shifts to them to show that the speech restriction is not content-based, is supported by a compelling interest, is the least restrictive means of promoting that interest, and so on.

Concerns about slippery slopes and dangerous administrators also arise: if we allow racial invective to be bridled, will we not soon find ourselves tolerating restrictions on classroom speech or political satire in the school newspaper? If we permit our fragile web of speech protection to suffer one rent, might not others soon follow? Moreover, someone will have to adjudicate complaints brought under the new rules. Is there not a danger that the judge or administrator will turn into a narrow-minded censor, imposing his or her notion of political orthodoxy on a campus climate that ought to be as free as possible?

Defenders of hate-speech controls, however, will see the controversy in quite different terms. For them, the central issue is whether society is free to impose reasonable rules to protect the dignity and self-regard of vulnerable young undergraduates of color on large campuses. Placing equality at the center of the controversy, they will see racist invective as endangering values emanating from the equality-protecting constitutional amendments and provisions.

Since these values are vital to our system of justice, they will insist that the free-speech advocate show that the hate speaker's interest in hurling racial invective rises to the requisite level of constitutional urgency ("compelling state interest"). They will insist that this interest be advanced in the way least damaging to equality. They, too, will raise line drawing and slippery slope concerns: If society does *not* intervene to protect equality from this intrusion, where will it all end? They will raise concerns about the administrator who will make decisions under the code, but from the opposite direction, wanting to make sure that the hearing officer is sensitive to the delicate nuance of racial supremacy at stake in these cases.

Differences between the two camps run very deep. They invoke different narratives to make their view of the matter seem the only one. As noted earlier, the free-speech defenders depict the current struggle as just the latest in a centuries-long succession of battles to keep speech free. They evoke a deeply stirring account, including early struggles against censorship by king and church. They see a history of book burning, inquisitions, Salem witch trials, and Hollywood blacklists. They cite heroes who in word or deed resisted orthodoxy and ignorance. This story is deeply rooted in the myths, history, and traditions of our people.

The minority defenders have their own narrative, however, one that taps cultural myths no less stirring than those invoked by the free-speech crowd. For them, the struggle over hate speech is a continuation of our nation's centuries-long battle over equality and brotherhood, one that includes early abolitionists who worked to subvert an evil institution, Quakers and others who operated the underground railroad, and 1960s-era civil rights protesters who marched for racial justice.

Each side thus wants not merely to have the balance struck in its favor, but also to place its interpretation of what lies at the center of it. Yet on closer inspection it turns out that the two stories are more closely connected than might be thought. The two paradigms—free speech and minority protection—stand in an intricate relation. Like lovers locked in a death embrace, each depends on, yet threatens, the other. Consider this interconnection and what it means for our system of law and politics.

HOW SPEECH AND EQUALITY BOTH PRESUPPOSE AND THREATEN EACH OTHER

Free speech and equality presuppose and threaten each other. Insult and invective, brought to bear by a powerful majority on a helpless minority, can oppress. They can harm directly, either through injury to the psyches of their victims or by encouraging others to take immediate hostile action (see chapter 1). They can also harm indirectly, constructing an image or stigma picture according to which the victim is less than human. But the call for respectful treatment itself can stifle and oppress, if taken too far. Imagine, for example, a community that enacted a rule prohibiting all expression that any individual in the group might find unsettling. This call for civility could easily lead to a bland form of groupthink and a stifling of dissent. Speech and equality are thus in tension.

Yet speech and communitarian values also depend on each other. As civil libertarians like the ACLU's former president, Nadine Strossen, point out, speech has served as a powerful instrument for social reform, something minorities, if they knew their own history, ought to know as well as anyone. But her counterparts point out with equal logic that speech, at least in the grand dialogic sense, presupposes rough equality among the speakers. Speech among persons who are markedly unequal in power and standing is not democratic dialogue at all, but something else—a sermon, a rant, an order, a summons—like speech to a child.

Speech and community are thus both interdependent and in tension; yet practical challenges require us to act. Minorities clamor for greater protection from campus insults, hate crimes, torts in everyday life, and symbolic acts such as cross burning. The ACLU and other liberal organizations demand that society refrain from enacting hate-speech regulations, and threaten suit if they do. The situation is often binary. If minorities demand a speech code on a certain campus, we can either oblige them or not. If the ACLU challenges a speech code, we can strike it down or not. What is a judge to do?

The usual approach in our system of politics whenever principles clash is to try to balance the competing values in some fashion. We hold the hope that an ingenious decision-maker can find a way to protect minorities from insult and invective while allowing speakers some liberty to say what is on their minds.

But the difficulty is not just the practical one of finding the right balance or compromise. Speech and equality are not separate values, but rather opposite sides of the same coin. Their interdependence arises because they are integral aspects of a more basic phenomenon, the interpretive community. Recent scholarship points out that communication requires a group of persons who agree to see the world roughly in the same terms. It presupposes a community of speakers and listeners who abide by certain conventions, who assign particular meanings and interpretations to words and messages. Without such an interpretive community, communication cannot occur.

The notion of an interpretive community explains the precarious interdependence of speech and equal protection values. Speech requires community—without it communication is virtually impossible. At the same time, community requires speech because it is our only way of doing what communities must do.

Yet, concerted speech can isolate or exclude a weak minority, just as majoritarian limitations on what is said can freeze social change. It is this precarious interdependence that makes the hope of balancing the interests of the two sides in the hate-speech controversy problematic. In effect, a judge weighing any nontrivial proposal for regulating or punishing hate speech is deciding whether to throw the state's weight behind a new interpretive community. That new speech community will have different boundaries from the old one. In it, minorities, gays, or women will be treated with greater respect, or less. Their image, their self-regard, will be treated with greater solicitude, or less. Their speech will be given greater credibility, or less. Terms and customs dear to them will be included in the lexicon, or not.

When judges make decisions with respect to speech codes, then, they are not simply balancing two discrete things, like Smith's desire to have a twelve-foot fence against Jones's desire to have more sunlight in his living room. They are deciding between competing conceptions of speech equality, between different worlds we might live in. This is at once a more portentous and difficult task than deciding whether the interest of a young black undergraduate in not being called a "nigger" late at night on her way home from the library "outweighs" the interest of the would-be speaker in shouting it.

How might judges approach this task? It is not the run-of-the-mill judicial assignment, like the backyard fence case. As we explain later, deciding between one speech community and another requires a dialogue. Judges have discussions with other judges or carry on internal monologues with themselves, all conducted through a set of conventions using words with established meanings.

These dialogues-about-dialogue will be heavily weighted in favor of the current regime. Thus, most radical reformers and members of movements that aim to transform the speech community should be under no illusion that judges can readily and fairly balance the two competing values—one established and entrenched, the other foreign and new. For judges to weigh proposed speech regulations fairly and dispassionately requires them, in effect, to stand outside their own interpretive community. They must be unsituated, have no experience, attach no particular meanings to words and arguments.

This is no easy task. History shows that when reformers have asked the dominant society to restructure itself radically, the response has often been incomprehension, if not ridicule. The would-be reformer is heard as urging that black be redefined as white, night as day, a thing as its opposite.

WHEN REFORMERS ASK TO CHANGE THE EXISTING SPEECH PARADIGM

At many points in human history, activists and innovators have asked society to transform radically the way it thought and spoke about a subject or group. Often the request was tantamount to a change in consciousness, requiring adoption of a new definition of the human community or community of concern, of the "we" in the "we are *this*." In most cases, this request was greeted initially with skepticism and disbelief. This was so in large part, we believe, because reformers were heard as asking for something that could not be said, or heard, within the current speech paradigm and was therefore unthinkable.

Consider, for example, society's responses to the early abolitionist movement. For decades, the principal response was ridicule and disbelief. Many whites, including some mainline church leaders, believed blacks were inferior to whites, childlike, and ill-prepared to assume the responsibilities of citizenship. Even a president (Franklin Pierce) reacted to the prospect of abolition in this fashion. In a message to Congress, he charged that granting blacks full rights was beyond lawful authority and could be accomplished only by the "forcible disruption of a country" he considered the best and most free in human history. He charged the abolitionists with appealing to passion, prejudice, and hatred. To be sure, part of the resistance to abolition was economic, especially in the South. But at least as much was conceptual, stemming from a failure of imagination or empathy.

Many citizens reacted to the early abolitionist message with surprise or scorn: What, free *them*? Early feminists and children's rights advocates met similar resistance. More recently, environmentalists, gay and lesbian activists, and animal rights advocates have encountered the same opposition. With the early movements, society eventually changed its paradigm or way of thinking about the group in the direction of greater inclusion. In the cases of animal rights, we will probably do so in the future. We think this contrast is general: proposals that entail a reconstitution of the human community or community of concern always spark much greater resistance than ones that do not, such as a change in the way we finance schools. The request that we change our speech and our thoughts with respect to minorities and women taps much of the same resistance that accompanied previous broad social reforms.

CULTURAL RESISTANCE AND HOW TO DOUBLE-CROSS IT

Consider the would-be reformer's quandary. We construct the social world, in large part, through speech. How we speak to and of others determines their places in various hierarchies of the social world.

The leaders of the reform movements just mentioned were asking for more than better treatment in material respects for certain people or things. They were also asking that these people or things be thought of, spoken of, constructed, differently. They were asking that terms like "human," "creature," "decent," "good," "nice," "precious," and "worthy of respect" apply to them. In short, they were asking for membership in the human community. Respectful speech, even more than willingness to rent a house or offer a job to someone, indicates the degree to which we accept that person's humanity.

Yet speech, including the reformer's, is paradigm-dependent. Unfortunately, both exclusion and inclusion are built into the very narratives and thought structures by which we communicate. In proposing rules that change the way we speak about women or persons of color, the reformer is heard as saying something verging on incoherent. The reformer, we learn, is asking that "us" be defined to include them, that justice means consideration of those others, that "nice" refers to those we have learned are "not nice," those who were excluded from the paradigm by which we first learned how to use that term.

Judges are no quicker than others to surmount their own limitations of culture and experience. In cases containing a radical reform component, even eminent justices often fail to appreciate the moral force of the new vision being urged on them. Years later, such cases are labeled "anomalies," failures that mar the reputation of an otherwise great jurist.

A judge is always free, within limits, to modify the current understanding of terms like "justice," "fairness," "discrimination," and "equal protection." But given the nature of courtroom encounters, which are intermittent and present their own peculiar combination of facts and events, that modification can occur only through a process of dialogue among the judge, the lawyers, and the relevant community. Such a dialogue is necessarily heavily weighted in favor of the status quo. Long ago, empowered actors and speakers enshrined their meanings, preferences, and views of the world into the common culture and language. Now, deliberation within that language, purporting always to be neutral and fair, inexorably produces results that reflect their interests.

Only a judge with no experience, history, or community—virtually with no language—could render a completely unbiased decision in a case calling for reformulation of the terms by which we define that community, change our history, alter our language. There is no such judge. Tools of thought primarily facilitate "normal science"—minor, incremental refinements in the current structures by which we see and rule ourselves. Law is no exception. After its passage, even the Fourteenth Amendment was primarily used to protect corporations and then later to rationalize a regime of segregation in which blacks were "separate but equal." The result of free speech, including the courtroom variety, is most often to ensure stasis, not to facilitate change.

Blacks, women, gays and lesbians, and others were not part of the speech community that framed the Constitution and Bill of Rights. They fell outside the original definition of "we the people"—they were not allowed to speak. Later, when they did, their speech was deemed incoherent, self-interested, worthy of scorn. Who would credit a member of a group composed of persons who—according to thousands of images, plots, narratives, stories, and songs—are stupid, bestial, happy-go-lucky, and sexually licentious? Words assign credibility and thereby define the community. Because those assigned a stigma find themselves separated from the mainstream, few judges will be on intimate terms with any of them. How many judges of Anglo descent are good friends with an African American, send their children to schools with more than a token black presence, attend social clubs where blacks or Mexicans appear in roles other than gardener or waiter? Excluded groups fall outside most judges' experience. What can they fall back on other than what they hear and read?

Much of what they hear and read comes, of course, from the law, an interpretive community of its own. At an annual meeting of the Association of American Law Schools, participants explored the question "Does the law have a canon?" Some answered no, the law has only cases, statutes, administrative regulations, and the like, all of which are the same for everyone, black or white, conservative or liberal.

But the law does have a canon. It consists of terms like "just," "fair," "equal," "equal opportunity," "unfair to innocent whites," "deserving," and "meritorious," all with canonical meanings that reflect our sense of how things ought to be, namely, much as they are. These terms reassure us that all is well, that our own situations in life are deserved (because fairly won), and that change generally ought to be resisted because the demand for it is incoherent or unprincipled. Many years ago, the majority of us learned what "principled" means, and it certainly doesn't mean the strange thing that reformer is saying! Words, once they enter the canon, freeze community, enabling us to resist transformation without even noticing how we do so. The suggestion that they are like us is heard as an impossibility.

When a reformer demands that we look at things in a different way, our first response is outrage or incredulity: what she is asking for simply does not fit our paradigm. What happens if the reformer persists?

Resistance is apt to spark predictable responses. We can refuse to hear what the reformer is saying, or translate the message into something else. We can declare that the reformer is obviously aiming to avert a particular evil, and then pretend not to find any evidence that the evil is in fact occurring. We can dismiss the reformer as extreme, politically motivated, self-interested, or bizarre.

Running through most of these forms of resistance is the idea that the reformer is imposing on us or our patience. Civil rights are fine, we think—up to a point. But with each successive demand, they tax our credulity. We have already admitted some of them into our schools, made places for them at work. Now they want to control how we speak, how we think! That goes too far. I'm entitled to my opinion and to speak it, too.

No longer victims, minorities become the aggressors and the majority the innocent victim.

Stopping them is now not only morally permissible, it is in order.

The point of canonical, deeply embedded ideas is to resist attack. The canon defines the starting point, the baseline from which we decide what other messages, ideas, concepts, and proposals are acceptable. Only moderate ones that herald minor incremental refinements within the current regime pass the test. All preconceptions—that women's place is in the home, that minorities are here at our sufferance, that the majority get to define merit—resist examination. This is even truer for the idea that speech ought to be free regardless of its cost (unless it amounts to treason, threat, defamation, plagiarism, violation of copyright, disrespect to a judge or other authority figure, deceptive advertising, and more). The entire point of the canon, after all, is to define what *is* a reasoned, just, principled demand. Because anti-hate-speech rules and laws fall outside this boundary, if one begins with a free-speech paradigm, reason fails and the status quo prevails.

STRATEGIES FOR CHANGE

Even though reform proposals predictably evoke stubborn resistance, history reveals a number of means by which reformers can nevertheless bring about change. These include rearranging interest convergence, tricking the trope, and the narrative strategy of the double-cross. Each of these tools is potentially available to reformers wishing to take action against hate speech.

Rearranging Interest Convergence

Societies rarely restructure themselves in response to a reasoned plea, but they do readily transform themselves in response to changes in material conditions. For example, the American workplace quickly accepted women once the slipping economic position of the United States plus the advent of information technology made women's entry both necessary and feasible. Reformers on behalf of women's rights had been advocating the virtues of equality in the workplace for centuries, while making little headway. Once the nation became persuaded that its economic well-being required women workers, change quickly followed. Derrick Bell interpreted the tortuous course of civil rights progress in similar fashion.

How will interest convergence bear on the fortunes of hate-speech reformers? With the sole exception of campus administrators (see chapter 2), municipal and collegiate hate-speech regulations do little to advance the tangible self-interest of powerful whites. At one time, the United States was engaged in competition with the Soviet Union for the loyalties of the uncommitted Third World, most of which is black, Asian, or brown. Then, it behooved us to be on our best behavior toward our own minority populations. We could scarcely portray ourselves as superior to godless communism, all the while visibly mistreating our own populations of color. Moderate reforms were enacted; the Supreme Court even upheld a group libel law in a single case.

With the collapse of the Soviet Union, the need for such exemplary behavior largely disappeared. Blacks and other minorities are relatively weak groups, while the forces arrayed against them in the hate-speech controversy are well financed, certain they are right, and able to command the legal expertise to bring and win test suits. Interest convergence is not a particularly promising avenue for blacks and others interested in promoting the cause of hate-speech regulation. Indeed, a certain amount of unanswered, low-grade racism and hassling on the nation's campuses may even confer a benefit on the status quo by keeping minority students on edge, never sure of their position, and reluctant to make demands on the administration for expensive structural reform of the way education is conducted.

"Tricking the Trope": Verbal Jujitsu

In the absence of interest convergence, reformers may employ other avenues for achieving redress. The first we call "tricking the trope." One can identify and enumerate the rhetorical strategies the dominant culture deploys to deny one moral legitimacy and portray one as extreme. Then one can turn these rhetorical strategies against the dominators. Martin Luther King Jr. was an expert at this strategy. Innumerable times he brought the lofty language of the Declaration of Independence, the Bible, and other cultural documents to bear in the cause of racial justice for African Americans. This sometimes stopped southern racists in their tracks—their own rhetoric and beliefs, their favorite passages from the Bible, were being used against them. King's most effective speeches and letters were replete with references to Moses leading the people out of bondage and to the political rights of all men, and reminders of this nation's commitment to brotherhood and equality for all.

In the hate-speech controversy, reformers might remind their opponents that our founding as a nation grew out of complaints over disrespectful treatment and petty annoyances at the hands of the British aristocracy, that the Pledge of Allegiance ends with the words "With liberty and justice for all," and that, more recently, the Third Reich prepared the way for atrocities visited on Jews, Gypsies, and homosexuals by first stigmatizing them and portraying them as less than human. The powerful rhetoric of the ACLU and other organizations committed to expanding free speech can be turned around. Why do undergraduates of color, for example, not have an equal right to go where they please without harassment and personal assault?

Double-Crossing the Narrative: The Counterstory

A third strategy available to reformers is the double-cross or "trickster" tale. In black history, oral storytellers and later black novelists and poets have used the double-cross to register their disagreement with a regime that oppressed and demeaned them at every turn. The Spanish *picaro* performed a similar function. The trickster employed slyness and clever strategy to win justice from a more powerful master; the double-cross was, similarly, a means to avenge unfair treatment.

Today, civil rights scholars, some of them critical race theorists, have been developing a form of legal scholarship that uses narratives or storytelling. Writers who adopt this approach employ anecdotes, chronicles, dialogues, and similar tales to analyze, criticize, and expose mindset. Some of these accounts take the form of stories from personal experience, illustrating a point about racial justice. Others take a different approach. Instead of presenting the minority perspective or experience, these accounts focus on some majoritarian narrative, for example the notion of white innocence, or that racial discrimination does not exist unless it is intentional, or that role modeling is a good idea. These counterstories are aimed at shattering comfortable majoritarian myths, such as that the nation is steadily marching toward racial equality. Derrick Bell's "Geneva Chronicles" are prime examples, but there are many more.

Could storytellers employ these tools to shake the complacency of organizations resisting hate-speech rules? Perhaps so. Irony, the demonstration of how self-interest operates in the current regime, and the "flip," the change of frame or perspective, are powerful means of introducing doubt or "suspicion" where they did not exist before. Minority storytellers have already begun the task of deploying such tools. Others could join in.

Cultural Nationalism

Each of the preceding tools—interest convergence and the two above-mentioned narrative strategies—presupposes that the insurrectionist group wishes to merge with the dominant society, but merely on more favorable terms. A fourth strategy consists of withdrawal, either permanent or strategic. The trend toward cultural nationalism among Chicano and African American groups is an example.

In the controversy about hate speech, we see the beginnings of such an approach. Parents of minority children, concerned about their well-being and safety at white-dominated institutions, often send their college-age offspring to predominantly minority schools, such as Howard University, where the atmosphere is more supportive. This strategy has the advantages of avoiding the need for hate-speech rules altogether, while building minority institutions and culture by allowing the next generation of minority leaders to develop in relative safety.

It is ironic that the threat of black flight may prove the spur that college and university administrators need to begin the serious process of assessing their own institutional cultures and environments. The University of Wisconsin, for example, enacted a speech code precisely at a point when dwindling black numbers on the system's campuses were causing real alarm. In similar fashion, the onset of defensive nationalism may supply a vital spur for reform.

We have argued that speech and equality, freedom of expression and the call for community, both presuppose and threaten each other. Balancing these competing values is complicated because the values are inextricably interdependent aspects of a more basic structure, the interpretive community. Judges asked to strike a balance between free speech and minority protection are in effect deciding the contours of a new interpretive community. They must decide whose views count, whose speech is to be taken seriously, whose humanity afforded full respect. Can they do so fairly and open-mindedly given that most of them come from the dominant speech community? This task is formidable, but urgent.

Most reform movements that asked society to transform radically the way it thought or spoke about a subject or group were greeted initially with disdain because the messages were heard as asking the unthinkable according to the communicative paradigm of the time. Every audience is part of some interpretive community or other, inevitably situated in some preexisting speech paradigm or other. Their deliberations have long been carried out through words already carrying established meanings. How unsurprising, then, that reformers provoke predictable responses. The rest of us either fail to hear their message, or mistranslate it when we do. We miss the point of their critique, then fail to find evidence for it once we do.

Hate-speech reform invokes a plausible constitutional paradigm, with its own history, case law, and genuine heroes. Yet prospects for change, through the courts at any rate, are poor. Because of the way we are situated and because there is little in the self-interest of elite groups to cause them to want change, reform of laws against hate speech is certain to continue to evoke sharp resistance. At some future time, the United States will probably join the majority of Western nations that impose limitations on racial incitement and invective. We will then look back on our current stance and wonder how we could have thought it principled.

8

"THE SPEECH WE HATE"

The Romantic Appeal of
First Amendment Absolutism

Does defending Nazis really strengthen the system of free speech? In *The Brothers Karamazov*, Alyosha, an impressionable young man, visits his mother's grave, where he has an intense religious experience. Transformed, he declares, "I want to live for immortality, and I will accept no compromise." Having discovered God—the most important thing in life—nothing else matters. Alyosha enters a monastery, devotes himself single-mindedly to his spiritual mentor Father Zossima, prays fervently, counsels the young, rescues animals, and effects a reconciliation between feuding schoolboys before the death of one of them.

In many respects, certain free-speech absolutists remind us of Alyosha. Until recently, the ACLU has held the line in every case of a proposed free-speech exception, invoking such doctrines and shibboleths as no content regulation; no viewpoint regulation; speech is different from action (you can regulate the one, but not the other); more speech is the cure for bad speech; and governmental censorship and self-aggrandizement are evils always to be feared and avoided.

But as legal realism began to arrive in First Amendment jurisprudence, more than fifty years after its appearance in other areas of law, sweeping aside the assorted mechanical doctrines and "tests," the traditionally minded, who much preferred things the way they were, shifted their ground slightly. Nowhere was this shift more evident than with regulation of hate speech, symbols, and monuments. With the publication of a number of influential law review articles and books, and the handing down of a trio of decisions by the U.S. and Canadian supreme courts, it now seems possible that cautiously drafted hate-speech codes will survive legal scrutiny (see chapter 2 for two approaches for drafting them).

But are they wise? Formerly assured that formalistic categories and doctrines such as the prohibition against content or viewpoint discrimination would hold, those who oppose hate-speech rules have until recently ignored these questions. Now, like an Alyosha beginning to doubt his faith, they are starting to hedge their bets and argue that even if hate-speech rules are constitutional, they are a bad idea and that colleges, workplaces, and other institutions should not adopt them, even if they could.

Earlier we examined two sets of policy arguments that opponents of such rules have advanced (see chapters 4 and 5). On the left, the ACLU and others have put forward policy arguments based on paternalism. These include what we call the "pressure valve," "reverse enforcement," "best friend," and "talk back" arguments, all of which have in common the insistence that hate-speech rules would injure minorities, whether they know it or not, and should be avoided for that reason.

A second set of arguments characterizes the moderate right. These include that mobilizing against hate speech is a waste of time—minorities ought to have better things to do; that hate speech is a useful bellwether that ought not be driven underground; that running to the authorities every time one suffers a minor indignity merely deepens victimization; and that minorities ought to toughen up or learn to talk back. Each of these arguments, which make up what we call the toughlove position, much like the ones the liberals offer, has answers. Some are empirically groundless, others assume a social world unlike the one we live in, and still others are inconsistent with other values that we hold.

Here we examine one argument that is neither paternalistic nor of the toughlove variety, but structural. Associated with the ACLU and others who take a relatively purist position with respect to the First Amendment, the argument holds that hate speech, Confederate flags and symbols, neo-Nazi marches, and similar forms of expression ought to be protected precisely because they are unpopular. The speech we hate, it is said, must be protected in order to safeguard that which we hold dear. The only way to ensure protection of speech that lies at the core of the First Amendment is to protect that which lies at its periphery. And this inevitably means protecting unpopular speakers: neo-Nazis, anti-Semites, the Ku Klux Klan, utterers of campus hate speech, and marketers of violent video games for adolescents and young men.

What can be said about this argument? It is commonly put forward by lawyers, legal commentators, special interest groups, and even an occasional judge as a reason for protecting odious speech. The argument takes a number of forms, each of which boils down to the insistence that to protect speech of one sort it is necessary to protect another. In all its guises, however, as we shall see, the argument is both paradoxical and remarkably devoid of merit.

TRADITIONAL FREE-SPEECH LAW: A FORM OF TOTALISM?

As mentioned, the speech-we-hate argument has been put forward by commentators, including ones associated with advocacy groups like the ACLU, as well as by a few courts. In no case that we have found has anyone attempted to argue for its truth or validity; instead, it has been repeated as though a kind of mantra: we must protect X in order to protect Y.

For example, the author of a recent history of the ACLU and a second book on the hate-speech controversy writes that the ACLU believes that "every view, no matter how ignorant or harmful . . . , has a legal and moral right to be heard." He explains that banning ignorant and hateful propaganda against Jews, for instance, "could easily lead to the suppression of other ideas now regarded as moderate and legitimate." The free-speech victories that have been won in defending Nazi and other unpopular speech, this writer points out, have also been used to protect rights messages and advocacy.

In two recent books and a series of law review articles, Nadine Strossen, the former president of the ACLU, echoes these views. "If the freedom of speech is weakened for one person, group, or message," we will soon have no free-speech rights left at all. Thus, for example, "the effort to defend freedom for those who choose to create, pose for, or view pornography is not only freedom for this particular type of expression but also freedom of expression in general."

In *Speaking of Race, Speaking of Sex: Hate Speech, Civil Rights, and Civil Liberties*, Henry Louis Gates and his co-author advance similar positions. Gates writes that when the ACLU defended the right of neo-Nazis to march in Skokie, a predominantly Jewish suburb of Chicago where a number of Holocaust survivors lived, it did so to protect and fortify the constitutional right of free speech. If free speech can be tested and upheld to protect even Nazi speech, "then the precedent will make it that much stronger in all the less obnoxious cases." His co-author, who forfeited his position with the Texas NAACP in order to defend a Klan organization, reiterates the ACLU position through a series of fables, all of which reinforce the notion that the only way to have a strong, vibrant First Amendment is to protect Nazi speech, racist speech, and so on. Otherwise, the periphery will collapse and the government will increasingly regulate speech we regard as central to our system of politics and government.

This type of argument is the favorite of not just the ACLU and its friends. Respected constitutional commentators have employed similar reasoning. A law school dean, for instance, posits that Nazi speech should be protected not because people should value their message in the slightest or believe it should be seriously entertained, but because protection of such speech reinforces our society's commitment to tolerance. Harvard law professor Laurence Tribe advances much the same idea. In explaining that there is no principled basis for regulating speech based on content or viewpoint, Tribe states, "If the Constitution forces government to allow people to march, speak, and write in favor or preach brotherhood, and justice, then it must also require government to allow them to advocate hatred, racism, and even genocide." The speech-we-hate argument thus takes on a number of forms. Some argue that there must be a wall around the periphery to protect speech that we hold dear (the center). Others reason that speech that lies at the periphery must be protected if we are to strengthen impulses or principles, such as toleration, that are important to society.

THE SPEECH-WE-HATE ARGUMENT

Many years ago, Justice Oliver Wendell Holmes laid the groundwork for the periphery-to-center reasoning by declaring, "[I]f there is any principle of the Constitution that more imperatively calls for attachment than any other it is the principle of free thought—not the free thought for those who agree with us but freedom for the thought that we hate." He urged that we should be eternally vigilant against attempts to check even the expression of opinions that we loathe and believe to be dangerous.

Later, in *Brandenburg v. Ohio*, the Supreme Court issued a ringing defense of an unfettered right of free speech. In vindicating the Ku Klux Klan's right to express hatred and violence toward Jews and blacks, the Court held that unless the Klan's speech is likely to incite imminent lawless action, our Constitution has made it immune from governmental control. And in the "Nazis in Skokie" case the Seventh Circuit's opinion reverberated with Justice Holmes's reasoning. In upholding the neo-Nazis' right to march in that city, the court wrote that its result was dictated by the fundamental proposition that if free speech is to remain vital for all, courts must protect not only speech our society deems acceptable, but also that which it justifiably rejects and despises.

Courts, then, make many of the same versions of the core/periphery argument that commentators do: without protection for speech we hate, the free marketplace of ideas will collapse; in order to protect speech that our society welcomes we must also protect speech we find repugnant. The argument in each of its guises is essentially the same: to protect the most important forms of speech at the center—political and artistic speech—we must protect the most repugnant, valueless forms at the periphery, including hate speech directed against minorities and women.

As we mentioned, the extreme-case argument is rarely if ever defended or justified. Rather, its supporters put it forward as an article of faith, without reason or support, as though it were self-evidently true. But is it?

Lack of Empirical Support

If protecting hate speech, buildings named after slave owners, racist monuments, and other forms of low-value communication were essential to safeguarding freedom of inquiry and a flourishing democratic politics, we would expect to find that nations that have adopted hate-speech rules and curbs against pornography would suffer a sharp erosion of the spirit of free inquiry. But this has not happened. A host of Western industrialized nations, including Sweden, Germany, Denmark, Canada, and Great Britain, have instituted laws against hate speech and hate propaganda, many in order to comply with international treaties and conventions requiring them. Many of these countries have traditions of respect for free speech at least the equal of ours. No such nation has reported any erosion of the atmosphere of free speech or debate (see chapter 6).

At the same time, the United States, which until recently has refused to put such rules into effect, has a less than perfect record of protecting even political speech. We persecuted communists, hounded Hollywood writers out of the country, and harassed and badgered such civil rights leaders as Josephine

Baker, Paul Robeson, and W. E. B. Du Bois in a campaign of personal and professional smears that ruined their reputations and denied them the ability to make a living.

In recent times, conservatives inside and outside the current administration have disparaged progressives to the point where many are now afraid to use the term "liberal" to describe themselves. Controversial artists are denied federal funding. Museum exhibits that depict the atomic bombing of Hiroshima and Nagasaki have been ordered modified in order to protect the feelings of military-minded viewers. If political speech lies at the center of the First Amendment, its protection seems to be largely independent of what is taking place at the periphery. There may, indeed, be an inverse correlation. Those institutions most concerned with social fairness have proved to be the ones most likely to promulgate anti-hate-speech rules. Part of the reason seems to be recognition that hate speech can easily silence and demoralize its victims, discouraging them from participating in the life of the institution. If so, enacting hate-speech rules may be evidence of a commitment to democratic dialogue, rather than the opposite, as some of their opponents maintain.

Paradox and Metaphor

A second reason why we ought to distrust the core-periphery argument is that it rests on a paradoxical metaphor that its proponents rarely if ever explain or justify. Suppose, for example, that one were in the business of supplying electricity to a region. One has competitors—private utility companies, suppliers of kerosene heaters, and so on. Ninety-nine percent of one's business consists of supplying electricity to homes and businesses, but one also supplies a small amount of electricity to teenagers and young adults to recharge their cellphones, which they use a lot.

It would surely be a strange business decision to focus all or much of one's advertising campaign on the much smaller account. Or take a more legal example. Protecting human security is surely a core value for the police. Yet, it would be a peculiar distribution of police services if a police chief were to reason: "human life is the core value which we aim to protect; therefore, we will devote the largest proportion of our resources toward apprehending shoplifters and consumers of recreational marijuana."

There are situations in which the core-periphery argument does make sense. Providing military defense of a territory may be one; ecology, where protecting noxious milkweed may be necessary in order to protect migrating monarch butterflies that need the plant for food, may be another. But ordinarily the suggestion that to protect a value or thing at its most extreme reaches is necessary in order to protect it at its core requires, at the very least, an explanation. Defenders of hate speech who deploy this argument rarely provide one. And, in the meantime, a specious argument does considerable harm. It treats in grand, exalted terms the harm of suppressing racist speech, drawing illegitimate support from the need to preserve social dialogue and interchange among citizens.

The harm to hate speech's victims, out on the periphery, by contrast is treated atomistically, as though it were an isolated event, a mere one-time-only affront to feelings. An injury characterized in act-utilitarian terms obviously cannot trump one couched in broad rule-utilitarian language. The Nazi derives a halo effect from other, quite legitimate and valuable cases of speech, while the African American undergraduate is seen as a lone, quirky grievant with hypersensitive feelings.

But, in reality, hate speech is part of a concerted set of headwinds, including many other cases of such speech, that this particular African American victim will experience over the course of his or her life (see, e.g., chapter 1). If we are willing to defend speech in broad social terms, we should be able to consider systemic, concerted harms as well.

The speech-we-hate argument draws plausibility only by ignoring this symmetry. It draws on a social good to justify an evil deemed only individual, but which in fact is concerted and society-wide. The unfairness of collapsing the periphery and the center as absolutists do would become clear if we rendered the argument: "We protect the speech *they* hate in order to protect that which *we* love." But not only is the argument unfair in this sense, it ignores what makes hate speech peripheral *as speech* in the first place. Face-to-face hate-speech slurs, insults, put-downs, and epithets are not referential. The recipient learns nothing new about himself or herself. ("What! I'm African American? I had no idea.") Rather, they are more like performatives, relocating the speaker and victim in social reality. Hate speech is about not the real, but the hyperreal, like an ad about jeans that makes no factual claim but merely shows a woman and a car.

Mistaking Principles for People

There is one setting in which it does make good sense to argue from the extreme or peripheral case, namely where human beings, as opposed to abstract principles, are concerned. For example, one sometimes hears it said that the test of a civilized society is the degree of protection it affords its least privileged, most despised members. Thus prison reformers argue that a society that locks up and warehouses prisoners under crowded and inhumane conditions with little opportunity for the acquisition of jobs skills, medical treatment, rehabilitation, or recreation is not deserving of the term "civilized." And so also with treatment of the mentally ill, juvenile offenders, the mentally disabled, and the desperately poor. Here, what we do at the periphery does say something about the way society values things like compassion, forgiveness, and the fair distribution of resources. But people, unlike abstract principles, retain their value and distinctive nature even at the furthest reaches. Human beings are always ends in themselves—there is no continuum of humanness. But our constitutional system recognizes not one, but many values. As we shall show, we cannot treat principles, not even the First Amendment, in that fashion.

THE PERIPHERY AND THE CORE

Every periphery is another principle's core; that is the nature of a multivalent constitutional system like ours. Principles limit other ones: X's right to privacy limits Y's right to freedom of action, and so on. Indeed, the idea of a constitutional principle, like free speech, that has a core and a periphery would be incoherent without the existence of other values (such as privacy or reputation) to generate the limit that accounts for the periphery. Thus commercial and defamatory speech, which have a lesser degree of constitutional protection than political speech, are subject to limits not because they are not speech but because they implicate other values that we also like. And the same is true of speech that constitutes a threat, provokes a fight, defrauds customers, or divulges an official secret. All these and dozens of other "exceptions" to the First Amendment are peripheral, and subject to limits, precisely because they reflect other principles, such as security, reputation, peace, ownership of ideas, and privacy. To argue, then, that speech must be protected at the outermost extremes even more assiduously than when its central values are at stake is either to misunderstand the nature of a constitutional continuum, or to argue that the Constitution in effect has only a single value, presumably one's favorite.

Moreover, to argue in such totalist fashion is to violate a principle that is inherent in our constitutional structure and jurisprudence: *the principle of dialogic politics.* As mentioned, law has not one value, but many. The district attorney wants the ability to protect the community from offenders; all citizens have an interest in not being randomly seized, frisked, and searched. A wants to speak. B does not wish to be defamed. In situations of competing values, judges attempt to "balance" the principles, trying to fashion a solution that gives the appropriate weight to each. (Not an easy task. See chapter 7.)

They are guided by lawyers and briefs arguing both sides of the case, as well as case law showing how judges have balanced rights in similar situations. Inherent in this process is what we call dialogic politics, the notion that in cases where interests and values conflict, people and principles (through their defenders, to be sure) ought to be made to talk to each other. In close cases, judges ought to heed both sides; lawyers representing polar views ought to be made to respond to each other's arguments.

But the totalist view of free speech admits of no compromise: one's favorite principle remains supreme everywhere it has a bearing, no matter how slight. This means that one is not obliged to talk to those other persons, not obliged to address those other values. If the whole purpose of the First Amendment is to facilitate a system of dialogue and compromise, this is surely a paradoxical view for a defender of that amendment to be taking.

Every totalist argument is indeterminate *because it can easily be countered by an opposite and equally powerful countervailing totalism.* With hate speech, imagine that someone (say, the NAACP Legal Defense Fund) argued in the following fashion: (1) equality is a constitutional value; (2) the only way effectively to promote equality is to assure that it is protected everywhere; (3) therefore, whenever equality collides with another value, such as free speech, equality must prevail. "We must protect the equality we hate, as much as that which we hold dear." Now we would have two values, the defenders of which are equally convinced should reign supreme. Each regards the other's periphery as entitled to little protection.

"Balancing" as we have seen is troublesome because it can disguise political judgments a judge makes sometimes unwittingly on his or her way to a decision. But totalism is worse—it gives the possessor permission to disdain entering the realm of politics at all. At least, balancing encourages the decision-maker to be aware and take account of the various values and interests at stake in a controversy. With totalism, one has no need to compromise or consider the other side. One finds oneself outside the realm of politics, and instead inside that of sheer personal preference and power-tripping.

With hate speech, the ACLU's totalist argument introduces special dangers of its own. Hate speech lies at the periphery of the First Amendment, as even its defenders concede. Yet the reason why hate speech does so is that it implicates the interest of another group, minorities, in not being defamed, reviled, stereotyped, insulted, badgered, and harassed. Permitting a society to portray a relatively powerless group in this fashion can only contribute to a stigma picture or stereotype according to which its members are unworthy of full protection—probably because they are, lazy, oversexed, immoral, stupid, and so on. The resulting stereotype guides action for teachers, police officers, and dozens of others, making life much more difficult for minorities in transactions that clearly matter: getting a job, renting an apartment, hailing a cab.

But it also diminishes the credibility of minority speakers, inhibiting their ability to have their points of view taken seriously, in politics or anywhere else—surely a result that is at odds with the First Amendment and the marketplace of ideas. This is an inevitable result of treating peripheral regions of a value as entitled to the same weight we afford that value when it is centrally implicated: we convey the impression that those other values—the ones responsible for the continuum in the first place—are of little worth. And when they are central to the social construction of a human being or social group, the dangers of undervaluing their interests rise sharply. This is so because they bear a stigma, so that they need not be taken fully into account in social deliberations.

Permitting one social group to speak disrespectfully of another habituates and encourages speakers to continue speaking that way in the future. This way of speaking—and thinking and acting—becomes normalized, inscribed in hundreds of plots, narratives, and scripts; part of culture, what everyone knows. The reader may wish to reflect on changes he or she has surely observed over the past decade or two. During the civil rights era, African Americans and other minorities were spoken of respectfully. Then, beginning in the late seventies and eighties, racism was spoken in code. Now, however, many op-ed columns, websites, blogs, letters to the editor, and political speeches deride and blame them outspokenly. Anti-minority sentiment need no longer be spoken in code but is increasingly right out in the open. We have changed our social construct of blacks from unfortunate victim and brave warrior to welfare leeches, unwed mothers, criminals, and untalented low-IQ affirmative action beneficiaries who take away jobs from more talented and deserving whites. And with Mexicans and other Latino immigrants, we have done much the same. The slur, sneer, ethnic joke, and most especially face-to-face hate speech are the main vehicles that are making this change possible.

THE ALLURE OF THE
CORE-PERIPHERY ARGUMENT

As we have seen, the extreme case (or core-periphery, speech-we-hate) argument rests on a little examined—and highly paradoxical—metaphor. It adopts a view of fellow humans as mere peripheral figures, and the Constitution as containing only one value. It dismisses the need for dialogue and makes the mistake of treating legal principles as though they were people and ends in themselves.

It treats the interests of minorities as though they were of little weight. It ignores the experience of other Western nations that have instituted hate-speech reforms without untoward consequences. What accounts for this argument's rhetorical attraction and staying power? We believe the principal reason is that hate speech no longer lies at the periphery of the First Amendment, as the ACLU and other advocates urge, but at its center. In former times, society was much more structured than it is now. Citizens knew their places. Women and blacks understood they were not the equals of white men—the original Constitution made it so, and coercive social and legal power reminded them of that if they were ever tempted to step out of line.

It was not necessary constantly to reinforce this—an occasional reminder would do. Today, however, the formal mechanisms that maintained status and caste are gone or repealed. All that is left is speech and the social construction of reality. Hate speech has replaced formal slavery, Jim Crow laws, female subjugation, and Japanese internment as means to keep subordinate groups in line. In former times, political speech was indeed the center of the First Amendment. Citizens (white, property-owning males, at any rate) *did* take a lively interest in politics. They spoke, debated, wrote tracts, corresponded with each other about how the Republic ought to be governed. They did not much speak about whether women were men's equals, should be allowed to hold jobs or vote, whether blacks were the equals of whites, because this was not necessary—the very ideas were practically unthinkable.

Today, the situation is reversed. Few Americans vote, or can even name their representative in Washington. Politics has deteriorated to a once-every-four-years ritual of attack ads, catchphrases, sound bites, and screaming rallies. At the same time, however, politics in the sense of jockeying for social position has greatly increased in intensity and virulence. Males are anxious and fearful of advances by women; whites fear crime and vengeful behavior from blacks. A high percentage of the public was never comfortable with the Obama family in the White House.

Hate speech today is a central weapon in the struggle by the empowered to maintain their position in the face of formerly subjugated groups clamoring for change. It is a means of disparaging the opposition while depicting one's own resistance to sharing opportunities as principled and just. Formerly, the First Amendment and free speech were used to make small adjustments within a relatively peaceful political order consisting of property holders and members of the establishment.

Now it is used to postpone macro-adjustments and power sharing between one group and others: it is, in short, an instrument of power politics. When neo-Nazis and white supremacists marched in Charlottesville, they marched under the banner of free speech—meaning, of course, hate speech aimed at Jews, minorities, and women who deviated from the role nature supposedly gave them.

Nothing in the Constitution, at least in the emerging realist view, requires that hate speech receive protection. But ruling elites are unlikely to relinquish it easily, since it is an effective means of postponing social change.

In the sixties, it was possible to believe Harry Kalven's optimistic hypothesis that gains for blacks stemming from the gallant struggle for civil rights would end up benefiting all of society. It was true for a time, at least, that the hard-won gains by a decade of civil rights struggle did broaden speech, due process, and assembly rights for everyone. Today, however, a stunning reversal has set in. Now, the reciprocal injury—safeguarding the right to injure others—has been elevated to a central place in First Amendment jurisprudence.

The injury—of being muffled when one would like to disparage, terrorize, or burn a cross on a black family's lawn—is now depicted as a prime constitutional value worthy of the highest level of protection. The convergence between black and white interests that produced the sixties lasted but a short time. Now, the ACLU defends Aryan supremacists, while maintaining that this is best for minorities, too. Fierce resistance to hate-speech regulations, which many college and university administrators are trying to put into place in order to advance straightforward institutional interests of their own—preserving diversity, teaching civility, preventing the loss of black undergraduates to other schools—generates a great deal of business for the ACLU and similar absolutist organizations.

In a sense, the ACLU and conservative bigots are hand in glove. Like criminals and police, they understand each other's method of operation, mentality, and objectives. There is a tacit understanding of how each shall behave, how each shall gain from the other. Indeed, primarily because the Ku Klux Klan and similar clients are so *bad*, the ACLU gets to feel virtuous, while the rest of us, who despise racism and bigotry, are seen as benighted fools because we do not understand how the First Amendment really works.

But we do. The bigot is not a stand-in for Tom Paine. The best way to preserve lizards is not to preserve hawks. Reality is not paradoxical. Our answer to the question, does defending Nazis really strengthen the system of free speech, is then, generally, no. Sometimes, defending Nazis is simply defending Nazis.

REFERENCES
(In Order of Mention)

Snyder v. Phelps, 562 U.S. 443 (2011).

Contreras v. Crown Zellerbach, 80 Wash. 2d 735, 565 (P.2d 1173 (1977) (en banc)).

Collins v. Smith, 578 F.2d 1197 (7th Cir.), *cert. denied*, 439 U.S. 916 (1978).

Virginia v. Black, 538 U.S. 343 (2003).

A. Leon Higginbotham, In the Matter of Color (1978).

Fisher v. Carrousel Motor Hotel, Inc., 424 S.W.2d 627 (Tex. 1967).

Taylor v. Metzger, 706 A.2d 685 (N.J. 1998).

Bradshaw v. Swagerty, 1 Kan. 2d 213, 563 P.2d 511 (1977).

Harris v. Harvey, 605 F.2d 330 (7th Cir.) (1976).

Haddix v. Port of Seattle, No. 840149, King Co. (Wash.) Super. Ct. (July 31, 1978).

Matal v. Tam, 582 U.S. ___ (2017).

Voltaire, Traité sur la Tolérance (1763).

Brown v. Board of Education, 347 U.S. 483 (1954).

Grutter v. Bollinger, 539 U.S. 306 (2003).

Danielle Citron, Hate Crimes in Cyberspace (2014).

Electronic Frontier Foundation, www.eff.org.

Doe v. University of Michigan, 721 F. Supp. 852 (E.D. Mich. 1989).

UWM Post, Inc. v. Board of Regents, 774 F. Supp. 1163 (E.D. Wis. 1991).

Wisconsin v. Mitchell, 508 U.S. 476 (1993).

Regina v. Keegstra, [1990] 3 S.C.R. 697.

Regina v. Butler, [1992] 1 S.C.R. 452.

R.A.V. v. St. Paul, 505 U.S. 377 (1992).

Henry Louis Gates, Let Them Talk, New Republic (September 20, 1993).

Donald Lively, Reformist Myopia and the Imperative of Progress: Lessons for the Post-Brown Era, 46 Vand. L. Rev. 865 (1994).

Stephen Carter, Reflections of an Affirmative Action Baby (1992).

Dinesh D'Souza, Illiberal Education: The Politics of Race and Sex on Campus (1991).

Henry Louis Gates et al., Speaking of Race, Speaking of Sex: Hate Speech, Civil Rights, and Civil Liberties (1994).

Randall Kennedy, Nigger: The Strange Career of a Troublesome Word (2002).

Sandra Coliver, ed., Striking a Balance: Hate Speech, Freedom of Expression, and Non-Discrimination (1992).

Nadine Strossen, Regulating Racist Speech on Campus: A Modest Proposal? 1990 Duke L.J. 484.

Derrick Bell, And We Are Not Saved: The Elusive Quest for Racial Justice (1989).

Laurence H. Tribe, American Constitutional Law, 2d ed. (1988).

Brandenburg v. Ohio, 395 U.S. 444 (1969).

Harry Kalven, The Negro and the First Amendment (1965).

ABOUT THE AUTHORS

RICHARD DELGADO is John J. Sparkman Chair of Law at the University of Alabama and one of the founders of critical race theory. His books include *The Latino/a Condition: A Critical Reader* (co-edited with Jean Stefancic; New York University Press) and *The Rodrigo Chronicles* (New York University Press).

JEAN STEFANCIC is Professor and Clement Research Affiliate at the University of Alabama School of Law. Her books include *No Mercy: How Conservative Think Tanks and Foundations Changed America's Social Agenda* and *How Lawyers Lose Their Way: A Profession Fails Its Creative Minds*.